CLAYTON

The Pittsburgh Home of Henry Clay Frick
Art and Furnishings

CLAYTON

The Pittsburgh Home of Henry Clay Frick
Art and Furnishings

Kahren Jones Hellerstedt

Joanne B. Moore

Ellen M. Rosenthal

Louise F. Wells

The Helen Clay Frick Foundation

Distributed by the University of Pittsburgh Press

Edited by Fannia Weingartner
Designed by Blagdon Smart Design Studio
Photographed by: David Aschkenas and
Herbert K. Barnett, Furnishings;
Lockwood Hoehl, Fine Arts; and Gary Lavin, Clothing
Typeset by Mangis & Associates
Typographic Service Inc.
Production Coordination by DDF&M Direct
Printed by Geyer Printing Company, Inc.

Library of Congress Catalog Card Number: 88-082158
ISBN: 0-8229-6905-X
©1988 by The Helen Clay Frick Foundation

Printed in the United States of America

Cover illustration: *Front entrance to Clayton.
This view was one of seventy-five photographs of
Clayton interiors taken between 1899 and 1902.
The tall-case clock and jardinières are still in place.*

TABLE OF CONTENTS

FOREWORD

Thirty years after moving with his young bride into Clayton, the first house he ever owned, Henry Clay Frick built in New York one of the finest town residences ever constructed in America, perhaps *the* finest to survive to our day. Interest in Clayton always will owe a debt to the enduring appeal of The Frick Collection, as the New York residence came to be known.

Visitors to Clayton who are familiar with The Frick Collection will be hard pressed not to see the former reflected, to some extent, in the glory of the latter. Clayton does indeed represent the first major step in the aesthetic journey of one of the most famous art collectors in American history. Yet, as Mr. Frick's daughter Helen understood so well, Clayton was more than just a beginning. Helen Clay Frick's conviction that Clayton stood for an exemplary way of life underlies both the purpose of this exhibition and the reason for opening Clayton as a house museum, a museum of virtually untouched turn-of-the-century interiors supported by records documenting nearly every household purchase made by Mr. and Mrs. Frick over a period of thirty-six years.

The prosperity that soon became great wealth never destroyed the basic kinship between daily life at Clayton and typical late-nineteenth-century domestic practices. Nor did the upheavals and tragedies that confronted the Fricks in the early 1890s shatter their faith in the future. Moreover, the Fricks' view of life remained fundamentally unchanged from their earliest days at Clayton to their final years together at 1 East 70th Street. Realizing by the late 1940s that she possessed an artifact that changing times had made extremely rare, Miss Frick, who inherited Clayton from her parents, believed that this place could speak to us in a clear voice of the way things were when American basic industries and the men who built them were just reaching their stride.

This exhibition anticipates the opening of Clayton as a house museum by two years. Its pur-

pose is to present a selection of the treasures of Clayton while the house undergoes restoration, so that they may be seen against the neutral backdrop of The Frick Art Museum's galleries before they return to Clayton's ornate and somewhat crowded rooms. Admittedly, the selection inclines toward paintings and furnishings that we, imprisoned by our own time, rate the finest; yet, there also has been a sustained effort to represent both the typical and the highly individual object. The result, we hope, is an honest picture.

Clayton, of course, was the home of a man who formed an art collection remarkable not only for its sumptuousness but, more importantly, for its consistently high standard of quality. Those seeking clues of early collecting genius will find them in this exhibition: the Tiffany & Co. mantel garniture (comprising a clock and pair of candelabra) and George Hetzel's *Landscape with River*, both purchased by Mr. Frick in 1881 when he was a thirty-one-year-old bachelor, attest to the sure touch of a discerning young buyer, albeit one whose stylistic preferences were not yet fixed.

Those seeking evidence in this selection of a consistent progress in the formation of Mr. Frick's collection, a smooth upward curve from nineteenth-century academic paintings in the early years to Old Masters later on, may be frustrated. Indeed, the formation of the Frick collection generally followed such a path, but there were detours and parallel tracks that tell of enduring loyalties as well as of a willingness to swim against the current.

One thing is certain: Henry Clay Frick loved the collecting of art all his life. He began long before his means allowed works of art to confer status upon him and continued long after his houses were furnished and his position as an art patron assured. He and his wife thrilled to the presence of art in all things they possessed; throughout their married lives they went to extraordinary lengths to surround themselves with the best that could be obtained. That this was so is clear from the exhibition; but why it was so—the source of the lifelong collector's passion—remains hidden among the mysteries of the human spirit.

The exhibition and this publication represent a group enterprise from start to finish. To Kahren Jones Hellerstedt, Joanne B. Moore, Ellen M. Rosenthal, and Louise F. Wells goes our gratitude for the careful scholarship and persistent effort required to produce the essays in this volume. All entries pertaining to ceramics and glass were the work of Ellen Paul Denker. Nadine Grabania wrote the catalogue entries on the Monet and the Hetzel. Sandra L. Smith dispatched numerous administrative and financial matters with a sure and steady hand. Linda Tobias and Nadine Grabania typed manuscripts and processed details with patience and efficiency. Not least, the editing and production of this volume were supervised by Fannia Weingartner, whose talent for disciplining literary effort and bringing cohesion to a pluralistic enterprise is prodigious.

The objects presented in the exhibition and in this catalogue are but the tip of a large iceberg. Upon Miss Frick's death in 1984, Clayton was found to contain more than 9,000 items, including vast quantities of china, glass, silver, and linen. Throughout the past three years the professional staff of The Helen Clay Frick Foundation has been ably assisted by the following volunteers whose devotion to careful cataloguing has prevailed over the tyranny of abundance: Mary M. Colonna, Ruth Garfunkel, Hazel Hood Kiley, Nancy S. Laitta, Donna Marshall, Marilyn O'Brien, Fame Craig Raisig, Kate C. Sladek, Carol J. Thompson, and Neil V. Yekich. Many of the foregoing have also assisted Joanne Moore in her continuing work of organizing the more than 700 linear feet of documents that comprise the archives of Mr. and Mrs. Frick and Miss Helen Clay Frick.

Finally, to Dr. Henry Clay Frick II and the Individual Trustees of The Helen Clay Frick Foundation we wish to express our thanks for their generous support of the project from the moment it was conceived.

DeCourcy E. McIntosh
Executive Director
The Helen Clay Frick Foundation

Pittsburgh, Pennsylvania
June 1, 1988

The Frick Family: A Portrait

Henry Clay Frick, the second child and first son of John W. and Elizabeth Overholt Frick, was born on December 19, 1849, at his grandparents' homestead at West Overton, Westmoreland County, Pennsylvania. His father was a fourth-generation Pennsylvania farmer, his mother the daughter of a prosperous landowner, miller, and distiller.

The formal education of Henry Clay Frick probably totaled no more than thirty months. He excelled in mathematics, and was known to have received his share of "lickings" for "monkey business." Frick showed no interest in farming, and when he was fourteen his maternal grandfather took him to the nearby town of Mount Pleasant and installed him as a salesman in the general store of Christian Overholt, a maternal uncle. The position evidently suited. While working for his uncle, Frick was able to attend the Mount Pleasant Institute on a part-time basis; there, among other subjects, he studied Latin. Later, he attended a ten-week preparatory program at Otterbein College in Westerville, Ohio. In 1868, he briefly hired out as a clerk in the Pittsburgh department store of Macrum and Carlisle until he contracted typhoid fever and returned to West Overton to recuperate. Viewed from a distance of more than a century, little if anything in Frick's youth suggests the sort of man he was to become.

Frick saw his opportunity in the coke-making business while working as chief bookkeeper at his grandfather's distillery in Broad Ford, Pennsylvania, from 1869 to 1871. The land in Westmoreland and adjoining Fayette County covered rich veins of coal that were being mined. The coal was then baked in beehive ovens to produce coke. Knowing that the recently introduced Bessemer steel-making process would require large quantities of iron, and that coke was essential to pro-

duce iron in modern blast furnaces, Frick anticipated that the future would bring an increasing demand for coke from Pittsburgh's growing steel mills. On that assumption he took the bold step of borrowing money from various sources and formed a partnership with his cousins J.S.R. Overholt and A. O. Tintsman, and the latter's friend Joseph Rist, to purchase a 123-acre coal tract valued at over $50,000 near Broad Ford. On March 10, 1871, the firm of Overholt, Frick and Company was organized. To establish the company in the coke business, Frick borrowed $10,000 from T. Mellon & Sons Bank (payable in six months at 10 percent interest) to finance the construction of 50 coke ovens. At the conclusion of the first year's operation, Frick had clearly emerged as the leading figure in the firm; the operation had grown to 100 coke ovens and became known officially as Frick and Company.

Through the economic panics and recessions of the 1870s Frick and Company not only survived but prospered. Frick served as senior salesman and spent much time in Pittsburgh soliciting coke orders. As the depressed economic situation continued and money became scarce, Frick, acting as the representative of local stockholders, succeeded in selling a small, publicly owned railway at Broad Ford to the Baltimore and Ohio Railroad. The proceeds from the sale enabled the stockholders to salvage their mortgages and made it possible for Frick to purchase readily available coal lands. More importantly, the sale to the B.&O. guaranteed Frick access from his coke ovens to the central

Henry Clay and Adelaide Childs Frick on their wedding trip in December 1881. Their itinerary included Washington, Philadelphia, New York, and Boston.

Above: *Henry Clay Frick's birthplace, the Overholt family homestead in West Overton, Westmoreland County, Pennsylvania.* Right: *In 1868, when this photograph was taken, the young Frick was working as a bookkeeper for his grandfather's distillery. He entered the coke business in 1871.*

transportation lines without fear of default by the indebted stockholders.

The metallurgical properties of Connellsville coke—named for the Fayette county town—became famous and the region was known as the coke-producing center of the world. Increasingly, Frick dominated the industry. In 1876, he was able to buy out his partners, who were under pressure to raise cash to repay debts of their own. Later that year Frick shrewdly loaned more than $8,000 to Daniel Davidson and Alfred Patterson, who wished to reestablish Frick's chief competitor, the coking firm of Morgan and Company, which had fallen on hard times during the recent depression. Earlier in the year, Frick had tried to purchase Morgan and Company outright but was unable to complete the arrangements because of a bout of

Henry Clay Frick (standing in the first row), and his traveling companions, fellow Pittsburghers Andrew W. Mellon (seated), A. A. Hutchinson, and Frank Cowan, on his first trip abroad in 1880.

inflammatory rheumatism (a malady that had plagued him since childhood). Frick's credit protected the property from other creditors and enabled the plant to return to working order. Unwilling to extend his credit further, however, Frick looked for a partner with sufficient capital to enable him to complete the purchase of Morgan and Company. In March 1878, Frick offered and sold a part interest in his business to Edmund Morewood Ferguson, a fellow coke manufacturer, and used this infusion of capital to purchase Morgan and Company. Having amalgamated it with Frick and Company, he reorganized both ventures into the firm of H.C. Frick and Company.

When the depression of 1878 receded and the Pittsburgh iron and steel mills once again needed ''Connellsville coke,'' they found that Frick was the largest operator in the region, and the one most capable of rapidly expanding production to meet the new demand. By the end of the decade, H.C. Frick and Company had made its owner a millionaire at the age of thirty-one.

In the spring and summer of 1880, Frick undertook his first transatlantic expedition to Europe, accompanied by Andrew W. Mellon and two other Pittsburgh friends. Together they toured Europe's great museums and private art collections.

In 1881, Henry Clay Frick met his bride-to-be, Adelaide Howard Childs. Born in Pittsburgh on December 16, 1859, Adelaide was the sixth child of Asa Partridge Childs and his wife Martha. The Childs family long had been established in Pittsburgh as manufacturers and importers of boots and shoes. Their residence on Halket and Forbes Avenue (now the site of Magee Women's Hospital) was considered one of the show places of the city.

When Henry Clay Frick married Adelaide Howard Childs on December 15, 1881, a local paper described the event as ''one of the most notable weddings of the season,'' and went on to mention the magnificent foliage and decorations, the ivory satin gown, the hidden orchestra, the ''exceptionally elegant presents,'' and the clarity of the bride's diamond earrings, a present from the groom. The wedding was followed by a month-long trip to Washington, Boston, Philadelphia, and New York.

After their return, the couple first resided at the Monongahela House, Pittsburgh's fashionable residential hotel. On August 15, 1882, Henry and Adelaide Frick purchased a two-story, vernacular, Italianate house in the Homewood section of the city. Located in what was known as the East End, the house was miles from both steel mills and

Adelaide Childs in her wedding dress. The wedding, which took place on December 15, 1881, was reported as ''one of the most notable...of the season!'

Social Mirror of Pittsburgh, an 1888 publication on prominent Pittsburgh women, described Mrs. Frick as follows:

The wife of Mr. H.C. Frick, the two or three times millionaire, is young and fair and charming. Her home in the East End is one of the handsomest in the city and she is the fortunate owner of carriages, horses, diamonds and all the beautiful things that money can buy.

The wedding trip was marked by the official announcement of the reorganization of Mr. Frick's coke firm. The announcement came at a luncheon for the newlyweds hosted by Andrew Carnegie while the couple were in New York. Already Frick's largest customer, the firm of Carnegie Brothers was eager to guarantee its access to the precious coke, and had been pursuing the possibility of a partnership since the fall of 1881. Frick, equally eager to find fresh sources of capital and an assured market, did not discourage the Carnegie Brothers' interest. On May 5, 1882, with the details in place, Frick reorganized his firm under the name of H.C. Frick Coke Company and made 40,000 shares of stock available. The Carnegie associates, including Andrew, his brother Thomas, their partner Henry Phipps, and the Carnegie Brothers Steel Company, purchased 4,500 shares, a mere 11.25 percent of the new firm's stock. The infusion of capital enabled Frick's firm to become the largest coke manufacturer in the world, and earned Frick the undisputed title of ''Coke King.''

The balance of power soon changed, however. Carnegie began to purchase the stock of junior partners and within eighteen months became the largest single shareholder in H.C. Frick Coke Company. Frick, ever in need of capital for expansion and preferring to have Carnegie as an ally rather than as a competitor, offered the Scotsman enough shares to give him 50 percent of the company. Carnegie accepted the offer. Thus, while Frick remained general manager and president of the company, he was no longer the senior shareholder in his own firm.

It was not always the smoothest of relationships. Carnegie, used to doing things his own way, often

downtown Pittsburgh and adjacent to still undeveloped woods and rolling hills; yet it offered Mr. Frick easy access to his office as the Homewood railroad station was but two blocks north of his entrance gate.

On January 29, 1883, Homewood, as the residence was then known, was ready for occupancy. Just six weeks after the Fricks moved, their first child was born, a son whom they named Childs. Two years later Martha Howard Frick was born, followed on September 3, 1888, by Helen Clay Frick. These were active years, filled with much social life for the Fricks and their children. The

circumvented the decisions of his younger partner. In 1887, Frick, exasperated by Carnegie's reversal of a labor policy, resigned as president of the coke company. As Frick prepared to sell all of his stock, speculation ran rampant as to the impact such a move would have on the coke and steel industries. Six months later, in January 1888, after an extended trip to Europe and a visit with Carnegie at his home in Scotland, Frick was re-elected president of the coke company.

The lesson of the 1887 resignation was a difficult one for Carnegie. Openly admitting that Frick was the best man for the job of overseeing his operations, Carnegie hoped to divert Frick's loyalty from the coke business to the steel industry. In 1889, Carnegie offered Frick two percent of Carnegie Brothers Steel and its chairmanship. Frick accepted the offer and almost immediately activated plans for reorganizing the firm. Within two years, Frick had united the various Carnegie interests includ-

ing mills, mines, and transportation facilities. The one exception to the unification plan was H.C. Frick Coke Company, still autonomous at Frick's insistence. On July 1, 1892, the Carnegie Steel Company, Ltd. was formed. The twenty-two-member board, for the first time without Andrew Carnegie (now content to enjoy the role of senior shareholder), unanimously elected Henry Clay Frick its chairman.

At the beginning of the 1890s, Henry Clay Frick and his family were riding the crest of success: the chairmanship of Carnegie Brothers had brought Frick increased financial gain, and national—indeed, international—stature. The family was thriving and Frick began to plan the complete renovation of his by now too-cramped home.

In 1891 and 1892, however, a series of events dramatically altered the lives of the Frick family. On July 29, 1891, five-year-old Martha Howard Frick died after a long illness. The Frick family

Mrs. Frick with her son Childs and her daughter Martha, 1885.

grieved deeply. They had her portrait copied and hung in several rooms in the house, and commissioned a marble bust as well. For the rest of his life, Mr. Frick placed flowers over Martha's portrait in his bedroom as he continued to mourn the loss of his ''Rose Bud.'' Throughout her youth, Helen Frick wore her sister's portrait in a miniature around her neck; Mr. Frick even had Martha's portrait engraved on his checks: a Victorian child's death was mourned in truly Victorian fashion.

Then, in the spring and summer of 1892, came one of the bitterest labor disputes in American history, the Homestead Steel Strike. The respective roles of Frick and Carnegie in breaking the strike are still studied, but the impact on Frick's life of events immediately following the strike is clear: he became a nationally known and, in many quarters, a passionately hated man. Within a month of the beginning of the Homestead Strike, on Saturday July 23, 1892, Alexander Berkman, a Russian immigrant and anarchist employed in New York as a printer and cigar maker, traveled to Pittsburgh to assassinate Frick. He attacked Frick in his office, shooting him twice and stabbing him three times, later telling a reporter for the *Philadelphia Press* that he wanted ''… to kill him that I might save and help the great army of workingmen all over the world.'' Views varied but there was general condemnation of the act. Even at Homestead, strike leaders expressed dismay and dissociated themselves from Berkman's action, rightly fearing public reaction adverse to their cause.

Frick rapidly recovered from his wounds, but a final misfortune befell the family on August 3, 1892, when, suddenly, four-week-old Henry Clay Frick, Jr., died. In the course of one year, the Fricks had buried two children and almost had lost the head of the family.

In the 1890s, as the Fricks sought to recover their equilibrium, husband and wife each followed his or her own pursuits. Henry Frick immersed himself in his work, traveling all over the world on business. Mrs. Frick concentrated her attention on her children and her household.

It was Mrs. Frick who oversaw the daily management of the house, which had been renamed Clayton. The maintenance of a twenty-three-room

A studio portrait of Mrs. Frick, 1895.

home was, in itself, a large task, given the amount of soot and dust endemic to Pittsburgh and its environs. Mrs. Frick directed her staff of seven in the campaigns to clean the layers of fabric that adorned the walls and hung at the windows and in the doorways at Clayton. Quantities of brass and silver had to be continuously cleaned and polished. As Helen Clay Frick recalled, ''My Mother was a meticulous housekeeper.''

As was typical of households of the period, Clayton had both winter and summer plumage. For summer, draperies and portières were removed, cleaned, and stored, and replaced by lighter drapings. Similarly, rugs were cleaned, rolled up, and replaced with rush matting; walls and woodwork were washed and varnished. In Miss Frick's words:

Early in November, the house was transformed by having the winter draperies put up and it took on such a cosy, warm appearance....

Mrs. Frick organized the activities, hired appropriate help, supervised their work, and approved their invoices for payment. This was particularly true during a substantial renovation in 1892. Writing to Henry Clay Frick, who was traveling, his secretary George Megrew reported:

She keeps herself very busy cleaning and arranging things about the place. And I really think she does too much for she gets so very tired.

The tedium of daily housekeeping was offset by the excitement of social life. Hosting and attending teas, recitals, poetry forums, dinners, and charitable functions occupied much of Mrs. Frick's time. Particularly popular were Mrs. Frick's Thursday afternoon bridge-whist games at Clayton. Among the regular players were wives of many of Mr. Frick's business partners.

Entertaining visiting dignitaries such as President Theodore Roosevelt and Attorney General Philander C. Knox, or First Lady Ida McKinley tested Mrs. Frick's managerial skills and reflected the Frick family's social standing. The luncheon that Mr. Frick hosted for President Roosevelt on July 4, 1902, was a grand occasion requiring weeks of planning and preparation. The house was festooned with the appropriate patriotic bunting, and newspaper reports told of the beautiful roses and orchids that bedecked the rooms. An eight-course meal that included melons, consommé, salmon mayonnaise, sweetbreads with peas, filet chateaubriand, roast duck, cheese and crackers, and dessert was served to the twenty-one male guests.

Above: *Chef Spencer Ford was one of seven servants to attend the Frick household, c. 1900.* Below: *Special events like the luncheon held in honor of President Theodore Roosevelt required detailed planning—from a carefully selected menu to the appropriate house decorations.*

For Helen Clay Frick and her brother Childs, the family troubles of the early 1890s appear to have become dim memories. As revealed by Helen in a childhood essay, their Pittsburgh was one of "azure skies and green lawns" peopled with loving family, entertaining friends, and congenial servants. Helen had nearly everything a child could want: dolls from France, ponies and carts, magic sets, a toy cow that "mooed," and even a playhouse that she shared with her brother.

Mr. Frick built the two-story playhouse on the Clayton property in 1897. Here the children could play and entertain their friends with lantern shows and small parties. It was filled with toys, dolls, and miniature furniture. Childs was the commander of the Clayton Cadets, a drill team comprised of neighborhood boys, who, in smart military uniforms, drilled at the playhouse and marched in local parades, especially the Decoration Day Parade at nearby Homewood Cemetery.

Henry and Adelaide Frick arranged a rigorous and expansive education for their children. Childs first attended the Sterrett School with the neighborhood children. In 1892, after the Homestead Steel Strike and the assassination attempt on his father, Childs was sent to boarding school in Cambridge, Massachusetts. There he was tutored by Clyde Duniway, who remained attached to the Frick

Childs and Helen enjoying a goat-cart ride at Clayton, 1892.

Helen, taking her favorite dolls Martha, Lissie, Louise, and Adelaide for a stroll, 1892.

household for several years. Eager to spend his high school years in Pittsburgh, Childs convinced his father to let him attend Shady Side Academy, from which he graduated in 1900.

Helen Clay Frick was educated in the schoolroom on the fourth floor of Clayton. There she and her good friend Elizabeth Frew were taught by the Fricks' governess, Mlle. Marika Ogiz. Lessons were conducted in English in the morning, in French in the afternoon. Weekly grades were presented to the parents, and Mr. Frick's penciled notations in workbooks that survive at Clayton

attest to his strong interest in Helen's education.

Childs Frick spent vacations with his neighborhood friends "the Bakewell boys," with whom he shared a great enthusiasm for the new sport of football. He was keenly interested in the natural sciences, and spent time identifying and tagging animals found on the Clayton property. Various woodland animals were kept in cages on the back porch of the playhouse.

Helen Clay Frick recalled spending her formative years happily amidst the great flurry of activity at Clayton in the 1890s. She took great delight in

the many visitors to Clayton, especially on the occasion of grand social events. In her memoir she wrote:

On formal occasions at Clayton, it was fun for me to peer between the bannisters upstairs and see the guests as they arrived, the ladies in their lovely gowns and wraps, the gentleman in their high hats and top coats.

Among her parents' friends, her particular favorites were Andrew W. and Richard Beatty Mellon who, after calling on her father to discuss some business, would climb to the third floor to pay a social call on her in the playroom:

I was fully prepared to serve refreshments which they were kind enough to taste or else pretend to enjoy while they sat in chairs much too small to be comfortable and at a table that was far from the proper size.

Left: *An avid fan of the new sport of football, Childs was photographed in football uniform in 1895. Below: Childs with his drill team of neighborhood friends known as the Clayton Cadets, 1897. Facing page, above: Helen, seated third from right, at a children's party on the Clayton grounds, c.1895. Facing page, below: Interior of the playhouse, built in 1897 and outfitted with children's sized furniture.*

Childs was keenly interested in nature and the natural sciences and participated in numerous safaris. This photograph was taken c.1898.

Helen Clay Frick was a frequent companion of her father on long walks, during which the two often discussed important matters. Indeed, Frick boasted to his friends about his daughter's keen business sense. It was Helen whom he always asked to escort visitors through his now renowned art collection.

As the nineteenth century came to an end, Mr. Frick once again found himself at odds with his partner Andrew Carnegie. Frick's primary interest in coke and Carnegie's primary interest in steel, the same interests that had brought them together nearly two decades earlier, would now be the cause of their separation. Numerous and complex issues, including the market value of their respective companies, the price Carnegie Steel was willing to pay Frick Coke for its product, and the validity of an unsigned dissolution agreement known as The Iron Clad Agreement, forced the partners into

battle. When reconciliation proved impossible, Carnegie, as senior shareholder in both companies, encouraged and accepted Frick's resignation as chairman of the steel company and president of the coke company. All that remained was the financial settlement. Frick knew that a buy-out would be impossible and suggested the consolidation of the two firms, to which Carnegie agreed. At a meeting in Atlantic City on March 21, 1900, the plan for the consolidation of Carnegie Steel Company Ltd. and the H.C. Frick Coke Company into the Carnegie Company was born. Frick received for his interest $15,000,000 and a sizeable distribution of stocks and bonds in the new company. Frick, who emerged from the consolidation a very wealthy and contented man, cabled to a friend, "Settlement made. I get what is due me. All well." One year later, the Carnegie Company was reorganized into the United States Steel Company.

The aftershock of the merger altered life at Clayton forever. With Pittsburgh no longer the center of Mr. Frick's business activities, he gravitated to New York. Beginning in 1902, the family had kept an apartment there at Sherry's Hotel, and in 1905 Mr. Frick decided to rent the house of William K. Vanderbilt at 640 Fifth Avenue. In 1906, the Fricks constructed a 104-room summer house, which they called Eagle Rock, at Prides Crossing, Massachusetts, on Boston's north shore. Winters in New York and summers at Prides Crossing left little time for Clayton.

However, the doors of Clayton did not close forever. So attached to the place was Helen Frick that, contrary to her father's preference, her coming-out party was held there in December 1908. Mr. Frick had wanted his daughter to make her debut in New York society, and when she insisted on Pittsburgh he was displeased. It was not until he received his invitation with "Papa, won't you please come to my party" written across it, that he relented.

Although the Frick family returned to Clayton through the years for special occasions, New York quickly replaced Pittsburgh as the center of their life. Mrs. Frick continued to pursue her gardening interests at Prides Crossing, and both Fricks trea-

Helen's coming-out party was held at Clayton in December 1908, despite her father's desire for a New York society debut for his daughter. She is seated at far right.

sured the company of their son's children, surrounding themselves with their grandchildren in their later years.

Following his retirement from the coke and steel industry, Mr. Frick pursued other business interests. Chief among these were railroads. His financial journals indicate that from 1905 on, Frick served as a director of "the Chicago and Northwestern; the Union Pacific; the Atchison, Topeka and Santa Fe; the Reading; The Pennsylvania, Baltimore and Ohio; and the Norfolk and Western" railroads. His holdings in each of these railroads averaged in excess of $6,000,000, and he was reputed to be the largest individual railroad stockholder in the world. He paid increasing attention to his philanthropic concerns, establishing endowments and contributing large sums of money to Princeton and Harvard universities, the Massachusetts Institute of Technology, the Lying-In Hospital of New York, Cottage State Hospital, and Pittsburgh's Mercy Hospital. Thirteen additional Pittsburgh and southwestern Pennsylvania organizations profited from his generosity, including Pittsburgh's Newsboys Home, Homestead Hospital, and The Kingsley Association.

In 1909, Frick established the Educational Fund Commission, later renamed the Henry C. Frick Educational Commission, to encourage teachers to pursue higher education and to provide the Pittsburgh school system with additional programs and equipment. The endowment was seen by the Commission's first director, Dr. John A. Brashear, as "perhaps, historically speaking, I believe, the first and only instance of an endowment by an individual, on a large scale of an American public school system." The Frick Educational Commission continues today, devoting itself "to the purposes of sound education and useful training in the public schools." Unlike many of his contemporaries, Frick often made these gifts anonymously.

A political career, the pursuit of many retired businessmen (including Andrew Carnegie), did not tempt Frick. He was an active Republican and contributed to the party on a regular basis, but although he was encouraged to seek elected office and was offered political appointments, he never

Designed by the distinguished Chicago architect Daniel H. Burnham, The Frick Building at 437 Grant Street, Pittsburgh, was ready for occupancy in 1902.

seriously considered public life. He preferred, instead, to exert his influence on behalf of his friends in their pursuit of political careers. It is said that Philander C. Knox, Frick's attorney and longtime associate, was appointed Secretary of State largely on the strength of Frick's recommendation.

The regulation of business seemed to be the major political issue that motivated Frick. He offered advice to presidential and congressional authorities when asked and exerted his influence when he felt his business might be threatened. His relationship with President Theodore Roosevelt is currently being studied to ascertain the level of influence that Frick had over the celebrated "Trust

Buster." It was Roosevelt who summed up Frick's patriotic fervor in a 1908 letter requesting Frick's assistance in sponsoring Commodore Peary and his next Arctic exploration:

[M]y excuse for what may be an unwarranted trespass must be my knowledge of your wide interest in whatever adds to the sum of achievement of American life.

Frick was unable to meet the President's request.

Much of Frick's time was spent in the pursuit of his first passion, the acquisition of art and antiques. His art collecting, begun in Pittsburgh, reached its zenith in New York, especially after he conceived the idea for a new Fifth Avenue mansion to serve both as the principal family residence and as a private art gallery. The house, designed by Thomas Hastings in restrained Louis XVI style, faces Central Park between 70th and 71st streets. It was conceived as a museum, and has been open to the public since 1935. In a sense, The Frick Collection is Henry Clay Frick's greatest legacy to the world.

In November 1919, Frick suffered a bout of ptomaine poisoning, but had nearly recovered when he began to display symptoms that his doctor described as an "organic affection of the heart." This "affection" was presumed by the attending physician, Dr. L. A. Connors, to be "the late result of the severe attacks of inflammatory rheumatism to which he had been subject in earlier life." On December 2, 1919, Henry Clay Frick died quietly at his New York home, seventeen days before his seventieth birthday. Adelaide Howard Childs Frick survived her husband by twelve years; she died on October 4, 1931, at Eagle Rock.

Childs Frick, who had graduated from Princeton University in 1905, pursued and developed his early interests in the natural sciences. He was founder and president of The Childs Frick Corporation, a non-profit organization dedicated to the study of paleontology, and served as a director and trustee of the American Museum of Natural History in New York City. He married Frances Dixon of Baltimore in 1913, and they and their four children made their home in Roslyn, Long Island.

Helen Clay Frick was graduated from Miss

Spence's School for Girls in New York City. She exerted great influence over her father and was able to persuade him to finance several projects she felt were worthy of support. With her father she founded the Iron Rail Vacation Home for Working Girls at Beverly, Massachusetts. Here, young women employed in the mills and industrial towns near Boston could enjoy a few weeks of fresh air and sunshine—so long as they did not bob their hair, gossip, or have male visitors.

During World War I, Miss Frick organized and financed a Red Cross hospital unit in France. She spent six months at the hospital herself, serving in whatever capacity was needed, including nursing and administration. During World War II, she dedicated herself to arranging for housing and education in the United States for British girls whose lives had been disrupted by the war.

Miss Frick's involvement in historic preservation began early in her adult life. In 1928, she established the Westmoreland-Fayette Historical Society as a branch of The Historical Society of Western Pennsylvania. Its mission was to preserve the artifacts and information on the life and the environment of Western Pennsylvania, West Virginia, and surrounding territories. The Society continues today as a separate entity, preserving the heritage of West Overton, Mr. Frick's birthplace.

In 1957, Miss Frick set aside 150 acres of her property in Westchester County, New York, to form the nucleus of the Westmoreland Sanctuary, a nature preserve and public park. Due in large part to her influence, gifts, and encouragement, the sanctuary has grown to 625 acres. It continues to provide a haven for plant and animal life and more than fifteen miles of public hiking trails in an area that, given its proximity to New York City, undoubtedly would have been lost to land development.

Miss Frick's central interest was in the collection and study of works of art. She served as a trustee of The Frick Collection, and founded as a memorial to her father The Frick Art Reference Library in New York, one of the largest libraries of its kind in the world. As the library's director, she initiated several undertakings, including an extensive research project through Europe and the United States concerned with photographing all the significant works in public and private collections. Also, the library served as a base for the American Council of Learned Societies for the Protection of Cultural Treasures in War Areas, a World War II committee that prepared detailed maps for the Allies indicating the locations of monuments and works of art to be spared from bombings.

To the end of her life, Helen Clay Frick remained devoted to her father's memory and his achievements. She spent most of her later years at her home in Bedford, Westchester County, New York, but returned to Clayton regularly several times a year for holidays and to entertain friends. She came home to Pittsburgh in May 1981, preferring to live her final years at Clayton. Helen Clay Frick died November 9, 1984, at the age of ninety-six.

Her legacies to the city of her birth include The Frick Art Museum, The Henry Clay Frick Fine Arts Building at the University of Pittsburgh, and Clayton, her childhood home. In the early 1950s, Miss Frick initiated plans for the National Trust for Historic Preservation to oversee the preservation of Clayton and open it as a historic house museum. Before the plans were completed, however, Miss Frick decided that her foundation should administer her property. It is by the terms and conditions of her Will, that The Helen Clay Frick Foundation is preparing Clayton to be opened as a historic house museum so that others may see what life was like for a nineteenth-century ''industrialist, philanthropist and connoisseur of the Fine Arts and his family.''

Joanne B. Moore

Clayton: Portrait of the House

In 1883, when Henry Clay Frick (1849-1919) and his wife moved into Clayton, he was thirty-four years old. He had recently made his first million, come to Pittsburgh from the coke region of Southwestern Pennsylvania, and married. By 1905, when he decided to move his family to New York City, he was fifty-six and a millionaire many times over. By the time construction began on his New York house in 1911, Frick was known the world over not only for his success as an industrialist and financier but also for the magnificence of his art collection. He was sixty-two years old.

During the years that intervened between the Fricks' purchase of Clayton and their move into their elegant new house at 1 East 70th Street, New York, the circumstances of their lives had changed significantly, as had fashions in architecture and furnishings. Although each house reflects its own time completely and is vastly different in style and atmosphere from the other, both demonstrate the careful attention that Mr. and Mrs. Frick paid to the decoration of their houses and to the quality of the furnishings within them.

Henry Clay Frick's early years offer few clues to his later attitude toward house decoration, and this is also true of Adelaide Howard Childs, who became his wife on December 15, 1881. A surviving inventory indicates that the household of Henry Clay Frick's prosperous maternal grandparents, Mr. and Mrs. Abraham Overholt, was amply supplied with many of the standard accoutrements of the well-furnished Victorian home, including a piano and an assortment of decorative items and pictures. (This is somewhat surprising, considering the Overholts' Mennonite origins.) It has been said, but never actually proven, that Frick manifested an early interest in art, decorating the walls of his room with prints and sketches. And

when Frick was only twenty-two, a report on his credit by an agent of T. Mellon & Sons, Pittsburgh bankers, noted that the borrower was "may be a little too enthusiastic about pictures but not enough to hurt." Moreover, Frick seems to have been inclined since early youth toward things of high quality. According to his daughter, he was always a fastidious dresser. He began to buy his own clothes at fifteen, and was apt to spend top dollar for fine apparel even as a very young man.

Adelaide Howard Childs (1859-1931) was raised in a substantial Greek Revival house in Oakland, a residential section of Pittsburgh. Her family was prominent in Pittsburgh society and business. Little is known about her early years, but Adelaide Childs probably received the degree of instruction in the arts and domestic crafts that was customary for girls of her social standing.

Nonetheless, when we look at the records of Henry Clay Frick's first venture into decorating, we immediately see abundant evidence of the interests he would exhibit in furnishing subsequent homes. After establishing his highly successful business in the coke region, Frick moved to Pittsburgh in early March 1881 and rented rooms at the Monongahela House, one of Pittsburgh's best residential hotels. Even considering that his rent included some meals, his $200 monthly payments were substantial for that time. And, unlike the proverbial bachelor indifferent to his living conditions, Frick within three months had spent $5,000 on furnishings, decoration, and works of art. He made his first recorded art purchase, a landscape by local artist George Hetzel, while living at the Monongahela House. He also bought furnishings of high quality in the most current East Coast styles, paying J. J. Gillespie & Company of Pittsburgh $105 for an "ebonized floor cabinet," probably the parlor

A winter view of Clayton taken in the 1890s.

cabinet in the Chinese style on display in this exhibition (cat. no. 1). Among the more than $1,000 worth of purchases from Tiffany & Co., New York, was a "clock set" for $850. From documentation of later repair and cleaning, we deduce that the "set" was the French clock and pair of candelabra in the exhibition (cat. no. 3). Clearly, Frick was already devoting time and significant sums to well-made, costly furnishings for his rooms.

This pattern was repeated when Frick and his wife turned their attention to decorating their first

home. The two-and-a-half-story house that they purchased on August 15, 1882, and later named Clayton was built between 1866 and 1870 on 1.43 acres of land. (This was eventually expanded to 5.5 acres, on which four additional buildings were constructed.) The exterior was not remarkable; it resembled many other vernacular Italianate houses built in Pittsburgh after the Civil War. Only the elaborate porte-cochère on the west side suggests that it was the work of an architect. [Lu Donnelly, *Clayton Building Documentation*, 1985, n.p.]

In 1881, Henry Clay Frick, then a young bachelor,
rented rooms at the Monongahela House, one of
Pittsburgh's foremost residential hotels. The rent was
$200 per month.

After purchasing their house, the Fricks remained at the Monongahela House while they directed extensive interior renovation. They hired Andrew Peebles, a Scottish immigrant who may have been the original architect for the house, to oversee work that cost close to $50,000—twice the initial $25,000 cost of the house.

Bills and letters indicate that Frick and his wife were both intensively involved in the remodeling. They purchased two recently published books on household decoration: H. Hudson Holly's *Modern Dwellings in Town and Country* and *Artistic Houses: Being a series of interior views of a number of the most beautiful and celebrated homes in the United States.* Frick wrote often to suppliers, sending measurements, explaining the finishes or materials that he and his wife wanted, and complaining about the style or quality of fixtures sent from New York.

Such effort for house decoration, particularly on the part of both husband and wife, may seem unusual; but it was not so for the time. Probably at no other time in American history has the home been considered so important, both as a formative environment for the family and as an emblem defining its owners' social standing. Writers on home decoration preached repeatedly on the momentous importance of furnishing one's house with thought and care.

While living at Monongahela House, the Fricks had purchased most of their furnishings from Pittsburgh manufacturers and retailers. Once they acquired Clayton they appear to have turned increasingly to New York firms. The relatively unknown concern of D. S. Hess & Co., New York, was chosen as "decorator." According to late-nineteenth-century practice, this meant that D. S. Hess not only advised on and supervised the installation of lighting fixtures, draperies, rugs, and wallcoverings, but actually made much of the furniture. (Clayton now contains the only known documented examples of this firm's work.) At least some of the furniture was custom-made for the house, as is shown by the monogram "HCF" carved in the crest rail of the 1880s dining room chairs.

Then as now the use of East Coast decorators conferred a certain status upon their clients; yet Frick expected more than prestige, he insisted on genuine quality. He wrote to D. S. Hess & Co. on January 20, 1883:

I would like your Mr. Hess to make a run out. I am very much disappointed in some of the furniture and mantels. [It is] really embarrassing to me to show it to my friends and say that it was purchased in *New York.* [emphasis mine]

It is impossible to judge the overall effect of the Fricks' careful decoration in 1883, because there are no photographs of interiors from this period and the house was changed extensively in 1892. Our only knowledge of the Clayton of the 1880s comes from archival records and the 1880s furnishings still in place today, and these indicate the careful selection of stylish but unpretentious furnishings. Dining room chairs (later moved to the breakfast room) exhibit the rectilinearity and incised lines of the then-popular Eastlake style (cat. no. 2). Overstuffed parlor chairs with long fringe and short, turned legs reflect the contemporary fashion for "turkish" furniture. Flowers, vines, and urns carved in deep relief, all very characteristic of the Anglo-Oriental style, adorn Mrs. Frick's bedroom furniture, particularly her bed (see page 28). And, while many of the decorative accessories were made in Europe, they were patterned after Japanese and Chinese models. Other ornamental items were imported directly from the Orient.

On August 15, 1882, the Fricks purchased this house, later known as Clayton. It was situated on just under one-and-a-half acres of land.

The furnishings the Fricks chose for Clayton in 1883 were in the latest style. Above: Mrs. Frick's bedroom, c.1900, with Anglo-Oriental furniture. Left: The stained glass window, ''Love in the Tower,'' originally on the main landing of the staircase, was removed in a later renovation.

Practicality and frugality are discernible threads throughout the correspondence on the house, as Frick closely monitored costs and reminded the decorator that ''Mrs. Frick wants parlor furniture covers that will wash'' [December 20, 1882]. We are reminded by the high chair (cat. no. 2), part of the original dining room suite, that this was a house where comfortable accommodation was made for the offspring, born between 1883 and 1888.

Pittsburgh Illustrated, a pictorial review of the city published in 1889, included thirty-two of Pittsburgh's best homes. Clayton was illustrated, but the simple Italianate structure, then twenty years old, looked decidedly modest and old-fashioned in comparison to the other houses. It is hardly surprising that in 1890 Henry Clay Frick and his wife decided to expand and remodel their house. In

1891, Frick chose a Pittsburgh architect, Frederick J. Osterling (1865-1934), to carry out the project. Osterling, who was only twenty-six at the time, had completed few commissions of note, and Frick's reasons for choosing him are not known.

When the remodeling was complete, the eleven-room, two-story Italianate house had been transformed into a twenty-three room, four-story mansion in the manner of a Loire Valley chateau. Popularized by Richard Morris Hunt and other American architects who had been trained at the Ecole des Beaux Arts in Paris, this style had been employed in New York since the late 1870s. Osterling's proposal, as revealed in the rendering shown here, was, in fact, for a considerably more elaborate edifice than was finally built.

For the 1892 remodeling, the Fricks once again

Frederick J. Osterling, a Pittsburgh architect, proposed this chateauesque remodeling of Clayton in 1891. His plan, suggesting a complete reversal of the axis of the house, was carried out in a much modified form.

imported decorating talent and furnishings from outside Pittsburgh, this time choosing the somewhat better known New York firm of A. Kimbel & Sons. The firm advised on the harmonious arrangement of all furnishings, supervised the work of the sub-contractors, and provided both special-order and ready-made furniture for the house. Other firms involved in the remodeling included: P. Hansen Hiss Company of Baltimore, New York, and Washington, for first floor woodwork; G. W. Koch and Sons, New York, for parquet floors; A. Godwin and Company, Philadelphia, for stained glass; and Matthews Bros., Milwaukee, for woodwork for rooms on the second floor and guest room furniture as well.

The geographic range of contractors was not unusual for houses built or remodeled by men of Henry Clay Frick's prominence. Industrialists frequently recommended decorators and architects to their business associates, thus forming an effective network of nationwide referrals. As Frick's business contacts expanded, so undoubtedly did his knowledge of decorators and manufacturers across the country.

To fully understand the Fricks' decorating intent at Clayton in the 1890s, one must go beyond the invoices that document purchases for Clayton and examine the attitudes toward interiors that prevailed at the end of the nineteenth century. The apparently overwhelming array of patterns, objects, and architectural detail that characterized Clayton actually followed clearly laid out decorating rules aimed at achieving a well-defined purpose. In the words of Clifford Clark in *The American Family Home* (Chapel Hill, 1986):

The ideal house [in the late nineteenth century] was a vehicle for displaying the civilized nature of its inhabitants. Houses were designed to read like a book whose symbolic meanings would be self-evident to contemporaries.

One might add that the house was meant to provide sufficiently interesting displays to be read not just once, but several times. According to authors on household decoration, every object had a meaning. Thus, Harriet Prescott Spofford, writing in *Art Decoration Applied to Furniture* (New York, 1878), boldly asserted:

The mere shape of a lamp shows whether people buy what their neighbors buy, or have any individual taste of their own to exercise.

The reception room at Clayton is a case in point. The photograph of the south wall (see page 31) reveals seven objects displayed on the mantel, five on the cabinet beside it, and three or four more on the center table. Paintings are hung one above another and one is even hung against a door. Every surface competes for attention. The floor is laid in a strongly contrasting parquet pattern and covered with flowered rugs. Below the picture molding, the walls are hung with damask in an oversized, exuberant floral pattern. Only partially visible in this photograph is the painted canvas frieze above the picture molding, a frieze of full-blooming roses entwined on a trellis. The elaborate Louis XV style chairs are covered with Aubusson floral-patterned tapestry and cabinet doors display painted pastoral scenes.

What was the intended effect of this room? To begin with, it is important to realize that at the time, decorating convention called for each room to have a distinct style and character appropriate to its function. The Fricks' reception room, which also functioned as a parlor, therefore conforms to a certain prescribed tone of elegance and daintiness. With its Louis XV revival furniture, floral motifs, and prevailing hues of muted pinks, this room met current requirements. Also, in line with fashion, the Fricks' reception room displayed fine objects imported from around the world, as would have been expected of a family as prominent and well-traveled as they were. Some years earlier a writer for Pittsburgh's *Bulletin* had noted that:

The...mantel and cabinet must be crowded with as many rare and costly specimens as the purse will afford, and certainly money invested in such shapes brings in large return of satisfaction. [January 14, 1888, p.10]

Objects displayed in the reception room included: the onyx mantel clock and candelabra from France (cat. no. 3); cameo glass (cat. no. 6) and porcelain vases from England; a ewer and stand from Austria on the center table; a painted tile from Germany or Austria; and what appear to be small ivory figurines, possibly from the Orient.

The paintings that crowd the walls reflected Henry Clay Frick's particular interest in art collecting as well as the family's general level of refinement. ''The Home is, in its way, a conservatory of art...,'' explained a contributor to the *Bulletin* on January 24, 1891. For nearly all Americans in the late nineteenth century, works of art were essential to demonstrating an awareness of culture. The type of art owned depended, of course, on the level of income. Moreover, Henry Clay Frick was not unique among Pittsburghers in accumulating works of art, as the *Bulletin's* editorial writer noted:

Our patrons of real art are...men of high financial standing and influence...[they] have been delighted to surround themselves...[with] choice paintings, bits of sculpture, daintily bound volumes, tapestry hangings ....[January 24 and February 21, 1891]

However, by the turn of the century, Frick's art collection was so well known that, according to his daughter, prominent visitors to Pittsburgh would make a point of coming to Clayton to see it. The *Pittsburgh Bulletin* of January 24, 1903, boasted, ''The superb art of Clayton has, in itself, rendered this beautiful home famous in the art and social world.'' (For more on Frick's art collecting see ''May be a little too enthusiastic about pictures,'' pages 62-66.)

The reception room, shown c.1900, was furnished in 1892 almost entirely with stock furniture from the catalogue of the New York firm of A. Kimbel & Sons.

In substantial Victorian homes the room considered most important for entertaining, and therefore the most sumptuously furnished, was the dining room. Clayton's dining room (see page 33) is no exception. The Fricks asked Osterling to design the entire interior, and the sketches found at Clayton show that A. Kimbel & Sons, the furniture maker, and P. Hansen Hiss, the woodwork supplier, took their cue from the architect. Documentation suggests that the only other room Osterling designed completely was the library.

The overall effect of the dining room must have been striking. All the furnishings were made *en suite* to match sideboards and woodwork, following the fashion of the time. The richest mahogany gleamed, set off by matte-finished, silver-plated lighting fixtures and furniture mounts. A frieze of green- and gold-embossed leather ran above the picture molding. No Victorian arbiter of taste could have asked for more.

Despite the fidelity of Clayton interiors to contemporary canons of decoration, there were interesting departures from the expected. At a time when many men of Henry Clay Frick's stature were building entirely new houses, Mr. and Mrs. Frick chose simply to remodel, and there is evi-

dence that they tried to reuse as many of Clayton's 1880s furnishings as possible. While Frick was on a business trip in 1892, his secretary wrote to him: "The doing over of the Library furniture was quite a success"; and a week later he wrote concerning Mr. Frick's bedroom, "Your walnut furniture [from the 1880s] is going to look well with the light colored walls and woodwork." Furniture from the 1880s was used predominantly in five of eight major rooms on the first two floors. The Fricks also chose not to custom-order furniture and draperies for the reception room, but simply selected standard items from the Kimbel catalogue.

The Clayton of the 1890s was stylish but not opulent by contemporary standards; the Fricks expressed their status conservatively. Describing a reception held at Clayton in 1903 for the United States Attorney General, Philander C. Knox, the *Pittsburgh Bulletin's* reporter noted, "Like all hospitality at 'Clayton,' it was characterized by liberality, dignity and refinement...."

A certain amount of resistance to complete change may be evidence of a sentimental attachment to the past on the part of Mrs. Frick. Her room is the only one that still retains its painted, grained woodwork, unchanged since the 1880s;

One of the watercolor renderings produced by architect Frederick J. Osterling in 1891 to illustrate his proposed remodeling of the dining room, intended to achieve a coordinated interior.

Rich mahogany, matte-finished, silver-plated lighting fixtures, and a frieze of green- and gold-embossed leather made the dining room, shown c. 1900, the most sumptuously furnished room in the house.

the furniture also is from the 1880s. Correspondence indicates that Mrs. Frick objected to any alterations to her room. Her husband's secretary George Megrew reported to Frick in a letter dated January 27, 1892:

Mrs. Frick's room is in such condition that I know it is a great mistake not to put new paper on the walls… I hope you will…speak to Mrs. Frick about the matter as soon as you return.

Even after the remodeling it was evident that Clayton was a home meant to accommodate children. Helen Frick was only four in 1892; her brother Childs was nine. The house contains a special children's entrance with a miniature sink and a simple oak hat rack. The new and remodeled

library furniture included a child-sized leather armchair *en suite* with the adult set. A special playroom was created for Helen on the third floor. Her room on the second floor (see page 34) was a child's delight, as she wrote when she was ten:

There are pretty flowers and birds painted on the ceiling and walls….If all the children had such a pretty room as mine, there would not be any of them sad or unhappy.

We see demonstrated in the 1890s the same traits that characterized the Fricks' 1880s decoration of their home: an interest in style, furnishings of quality, and artistic effect; and a commitment to comfortable accommodation for every family member, to practicality and to thrift.

With walls painted with cascading roses and a ceiling of blue sky, Helen Clay Frick's room, c. 1900, was a young girl's delight.

It was not long after the 1892 remodeling that Clayton once again seemed too cramped and too modest. More space was needed for a rapidly expanding art collection, for entertaining, and for staff to handle the increasing social demands on the family. Henry Clay Frick's art collection burgeoned after 1895, and around 1897 he made plans to build an art gallery connected to the parlor of Clayton. He also contracted shortly thereafter for plans for a new wing in the English Tudor style almost as large as Clayton itself. To be added to the rear of the house, the wing included a ballroom, a new kitchen, and rooms for more than double the handful of servants then living at Clayton.

In the end, however, these plans were not carried out. Instead, Frick decided to build a new house. As Helen Clay Frick would later explain in her introductory essay to *The Frick Collection* (1949), it was the art collection that ''caused him to have plans drawn up for a larger house [on] property known as Gun's Hill...on Beechwood Boulevard in Pittsburgh.'' Yet, this too was never built. Miss Frick explained, ''further study revealed that the smoke from Homestead would undoubtedly be injurious to the pictures....''

In any case, for the time being the Fricks decided to redecorate Clayton. For this job they hired the well-known firm of Cottier and Company, New York, which was to decorate their next two homes

as well. Although itemized documentation of the firm's work at Clayton is lacking, we know that the overall cost of the decoration was more than $100,000. It appears that Cottier replaced 1880s stained glass with classically inspired windows and recovered walls with plainer fabrics than the floral damasks and striped and painted silks that had been used before.

The intent of the redecoration was the reduction of ornamental detail, reflecting the dramatic shift in decorating taste that had occurred shortly before the turn of the century. Reforms in household decoration, codified in 1897 in *The Decoration of Houses* by Edith Wharton and Ogden Codman, Jr., had banished Victorian clutter and reshaped the look of the fashionable house. The Cottier redecoration of Clayton demonstrates the Fricks' interest in keeping abreast of current decorating fashion, although to our eyes the alterations failed to change the essential character of this late Victorian dwelling. It was not until the construction and furnishing of subsequent homes that the shift in the Fricks' taste became obvious.

As early as 1902, the Fricks had begun to spend time away from Clayton. From then on, they spent summers at Prides Crossing on Boston's north shore, first in a rented house, then at Eagle Rock, a neo-Georgian mansion they built for themselves. In 1902, Henry Clay Frick rented an apartment for

In 1906 the Fricks built a summer house at Prides Crossing, Massachusetts, and filled it with antiques and fine art. The house contained 104 rooms. Shown here is the music room.

the family at Sherry's—a residential hotel in New York. Frick was no stranger to New York, but once released from day-to-day business responsibilities in Pittsburgh, he chose to spend more time in the larger city.

Three years later, the Fricks rented from George W. Vanderbilt the famous house at 640 Fifth Avenue, built by William H. Vanderbilt between 1879 and 1882. As one of the first houses designed by Richard Morris Hunt in the chateauesque style, this American palace may well have influenced the 1892 remodeling of Clayton.

Described in its time as "Medicean," the opulent Vanderbilt mansion represented a significant departure from stylish, but homey, Clayton. The

gap between the Fricks' first house and their next two houses became even more marked. The 104-room Eagle Rock built in 1906 was furnished largely with genuine and reproduction English and French eighteenth-century antiques. These were set in rooms with plain walls in accordance with the new emphasis on simplicity and authenticity in interior decoration.

The house the Fricks built at 1 East 70th Street in New York between 1911 and 1914 (open to the public since 1935 as The Frick Collection) was the ultimate expression of restrained classicism, both in its architecture and interior furnishings. By this time Frick possessed a world-renowned art collection, which he was determined to make accessible

The house that the Fricks built at 1 East 70th Street, New York, has been called the ultimate townhouse. Open to the public since 1935, it is now known as The Frick Collection. The view at left captures the elegance of the interiors.

to the public following his death. Helen Clay Frick recalled that his inspiration was the Wallace Collection in London, which he had visited on his first trip to Europe in 1880. The house at 1 East 70th Street was planned from the beginning to receive the public.

The majority of the objects in this exhibition and catalogue derive from the more private phase of the family's life during their years at Clayton. But taken together, the assemblage of furniture, ceramics, silver, and glass suggest the evolving taste of Henry Clay and Adelaide Frick, as well as their enduring interest in quality and decorating fashion, from Henry Frick's bachelor rooms at the Monongahela House, to the comfortable family home, Clayton, to the regal splendor of the house in New York.

Ellen M. Rosenthal

Selection of Furnishings from the Exhibition

1. Parlor Cabinet, c.1880

Maker: Unknown, possibly from New York
Ebonized cherry, gilt decoration, marquetry plaque
  of various woods, mirror glass, brass
H: 84¾ in. (215 cm.)
Unmarked
Purchased: J.J. Gillespie & Co., Pittsburgh,
  Pennsylvania, February 19, 1881

While the impact of Oriental crafts on American design and interior decoration is readily acknowledged by decorative art historians today, it is Japan that is most frequently cited as the source of inspiration. According to Ellen Paul Denker in *After the Chinese Taste*, while "Anglo-Japanese" was a term favored by designers in the late nineteenth century, they in fact frequently drew design inspiration from Chinese forms. She postulates that "the craze for things Japanese and the menial position of Chinese workers in Western society at the time led writers...to ignore the influence of the Chinese."

The parlor cabinet pictured here is clearly modeled on Chinese forms: the cresting suggests a Chinese pagoda and the ebonized surface evokes Chinese lacquer-work. The incised and gilt decorative panels with insects, flowers, and bamboo are more generally Oriental in feeling.

We believe that the cabinet was purchased by Henry Clay Frick on February 19, 1881, from J. J. Gillespie & Co., Pittsburgh, for his bachelor rooms at the Monongahela House. The invoice reads "One Ebony Floor Cabinet 105.00."

Intended for the display of collections of assorted decorative treasures, the cabinet must have been a useful furnishing for Frick, who was in the process of accumulating accessories from Pittsburgh and New York shops.

J. J. Gillespie & Co., which remains in operation, is known primarily as a fine arts gallery. In the nineteenth century the firm offered a greater variety of home furnishings. An undated nineteenth-century photograph shows frames, furniture, sculpture, porcelain, and art—all undoubtedly imported from outside Pittsburgh. The origin of this cabinet is not known. Presumably, given its place of purchase and stylishness, it came from an East Coast city, most likely New York. E. M. R.

1.

2. Armchair, Child's High Chair, 1883

Maker: D. S. Hess & Co., New York,
  New York (1873-1889)
Mahogany, leather
H: (Armchair) 38⅞ in. (98.8 cm.); (High Chair) 35⅛ in.
  (89.3 cm.)
Unmarked

On January 30, 1883, Henry Clay Frick wrote to Messrs. D. S. Hess & Co., New York City that:

The dining room chairs are entirely satisfactory. [However], I am very much disappointed in...some of the furniture and mantels.

In the absence of invoices detailing the work done for the Fricks by D. S. Hess & Co., this letter is the source of our knowledge that the firm made the

2.

furniture for Clayton in the 1880s. We surmise that the chairs pictured here are the dining room chairs referred to. New dining room furniture was made in 1892 and these chairs have been in use in the breakfast room since then.

D. S. Hess & Co., is not well known today; none of the firm's work appears in any recent publications on nineteenth-century American furniture. Neither, apparently, was the company noted at the time. First mention of the concern appears in New York City directories in 1873-74 when ''David S. Hess, cabinetmaker'' is listed at 178 Wooster St. Hess moved three times in the ensuing seven years, changing his listing to ''David S. Hess, furniture.'' In 1883-84, he opened a second office at 145 Eleventh Avenue and in 1884-85 moved his first office to a more prestigious location on Broadway. The firm was not listed as D. S. Hess & Co. until 1888-89, the last year it was listed in the directories. Without further documentation, one must infer that D. S. Hess & Co. experienced no more than a brief flutter of success.

From these chairs, however, one can see that Hess made furniture in the latest taste. They bear a marked resemblance to drawings shown in Harriet Spofford's *Art Decoration Applied to Furniture*, 1878, based on the dicta of Charles Locke Eastlake, the English proponent of design reform. In his book *Hints on Household Taste*, first published in London in 1868, Eastlake called for ''plain and

straightforward'' construction. He suggested turned legs, squared-off composition and solid grained woods.

Early photographs and inventories indicate that two high chairs were part of this set. Identical in decoration, though not in scale, to the chairs made for Mr. and Mrs. Frick, the high chair pictured here is a touching reminder of how central the children were to life at Clayton.

Miss Frick replaced the leather on these chairs in 1953 as part of her initial effort to prepare Clayton for its opening to the public.   E. M. R.

3. *Clock and Candelabra, c.1881*

Maker: Unknown, probably French

Onyx, gilt bronze

H: (Candelabra) 27 in. (70.0 cm.); (Clock) 27¾ in. (70.5 cm.)

Marked on clock movement: *5607/TIFFANY & CO./ New York* and on clock dial: *TIFFANY & COMP.*

Purchased: Tiffany & Co., New York, New York, March 15, 1881

Executed in the classically inspired Louis XVI style with deeply veined onyx body and cast ormolu ornamentation, this clock and candelabra are a sophisticated expression of late-nineteenth-century design. The decorative elements—putti, festoons of flowers and leaves, and bands of low relief ornamentation—clearly recall eighteenth-century models; however, the decidedly

3.

nineteenth-century arrangement of these features and the use of cast elements resembling appliquéd and fringed lambrequins from the late 1870s confirm a date close to the time of purchase.

The mark Tiffany & Co. on the clock face indicates that the set was sold at that firm's retail store. By 1870, when Tiffany opened its Union Square outlet in New York, it had become well known as a luxury store carrying sumptuous merchandise from all over the world. Style and technique suggest that this clock and candelabra were imported from France.

Clock and candelabra sets, used for mantel garniture, were ubiquitous in fashionable homes of the late nineteenth century. Even so, it is surprising that Henry Clay Frick as a bachelor purchased this ''clock set'' from Tiffany & Co., New York, for $850 on March 15, 1881, soon after renting rooms at the Monongahela House, a residential hotel. The purchase manifests Frick's early interest in objects of high quality.

Nearly twenty years after its purchase, the clock and candelabra were still displayed prominently on the mantel of the reception room, surrounded by French paintings of the mid-nineteenth century and reproduction furniture in the Louis XV style. In Miss Frick's time the set was displayed on the parlor mantel, where it remains today. E. M. R.

4.

4. *Vase (One of a Pair), 1868-1900*

Maker: Unknown, Japanese
Bronze, enamels, gold
H: 7⅝ in. (19.4 cm.)
Impressed on bottom with stylized mountains and
  Japanese characters within an oval

Westerners have been fascinated by Oriental handcrafts since the sixteenth century. However, because Japan was closed to trade with the West until 1854, it was not until the second half of the nineteenth century that Japanese decorative and fine arts reached Western countries in large quantity and become a powerful influence on European and American decoration and design.

Clayton was typical of many American homes in the last quarter of the nineteenth century in that it boasted both Japanese-made and Japanese-influenced furnishings. In 1878, Harriet Spofford, writer on home decoration, recommended Japanese furniture, rush matting, and decorative accessories for interiors of nearly any decor. Photographs of American interiors from the 1870s and 1880s show abundant use of fans, porcelains, kimonos, screens, and other Japanese items.

The American fondness for things Japanese was as much in evidence in Pittsburgh as elsewhere. On January 14, 1888, the firm of Wm. Haslage & Sons on Market Square, Pittsburgh, advertised in the *Bulletin*, that it was the sole agent for ''Fine Groceries, Teas and *Japanese Goods*.'' In a February 11, 1888, issue of the same paper, a writer on home decoration recommended that a ''large Japanese Kakemono and tapestry cross-stripe portières of Oriental pattern'' would be perfect for a little drawing-room.

We do not know for sure when the Fricks purchased or were given the Japanese bronze vases pictured here. Given the predilection for Oriental-influenced wares apparent in the 1880s decoration of their house, it is likely that these vases were acquired in the early period at Clayton; they appear in a photograph of the library sitting room taken around 1900.

The vases are ornamented to suggest an autumnal theme with flying sparrows and falling Japanese maple leaves on the front and spider webs and insects on the back. Ornamental detail is in high relief and highlighted with red and brown enamel and gold. The shape of the vases resembles that of old Korean ceramic vases. While we do not know their exact date of manufacture, it is certain that they were produced in the Meiji era (c. 1868-1912), when large quantities of non-utilitarian bronze objects were made for export. The typically Japanese motifs and highlighting techniques that appear on these vases were the same as the ones that had influenced the Western-made products that the Fricks purchased around this time, including a tea service by Whiting with applied copper decoration (cat. no. 7) and the dessert plates by Mintons (cat. no. 5).   E. M. R.

5. *Dessert Plate (from a Service for Ten), 1880*

Maker: Mintons Limited, Stoke-on-Trent, England (1796-1968)

Porcelain, enameled and gilded

Diam: 6⁹⁄₁₆ in. (16.8 cm.)

Marks printed in purple overglaze include: a crown over a globe with *MINTONS,* all above a ribbon identifying *Messrs Caldwell & Co./PHILADELPHIA* (the retailers); impressed underglaze *MINTONS* with three factory symbols; craftsmen's notations overglaze

Purchased: Messrs. Caldwell & Co., Philadelphia, Pennsylvania, c. 1880

The ceramics of earliest date at Clayton, many of them possibly received as wedding presents, exhibit the taste for things Japanese prevalent in Europe and America between 1875 and 1885. This derived from the sensation created by the display of the applied arts of Japan at the 1862 London and 1867 Paris exhibitions. For factory production of this period, Oriental motifs provided perhaps the greatest influence at firms like Mintons, which produced stylish goods for a wealthy clientele.

Porcelain was first made by Thomas Minton at Stoke in 1796. In 1849, Leon Arnoux, a Frenchman, became art director under Thomas Minton's son Herbert. During his forty-three years in that role,

Arnoux brought a number of important French designers and decorators to the firm.

Although these dessert plates were produced as useful decorative wares rather than art wares, the stamp of design genius can be seen clearly in the juxtaposition of stylized motif and brilliant coloring.

E. P. D.

5.

6. *Vase, 1880-1890*

Maker: Attributed to Thomas Webb and Sons, Stourbridge, England (1837-1919)

Colored glass, cased and cameo-engraved

H: 8½ in. (21.5 cm.)

Unmarked

Although the art of cameo glass is more than 2,000 years old, it has not been practiced continuously in any one culture for long periods of time. Based on the ancient process of creating decoration by cutting through contrasting layers of stone, this technique, when applied to glass, allowed the use of a wider variety of colors than could have been afforded by natural materials.

Wedgwood's popular reproductions in stoneware of the famous Portland Vase provided the catalyst for the development of cameo engraving in the English glass industry when interest in classical art revived during the late nineteenth century. The acclaim accorded John Northwood for his version of the vase in glass, finished in 1876 after three years of painstaking work, led to a demand for cameo glass executed in a variety of styles, including classical, aesthetic, Persian, and Oriental.

The center of cameo glass production in England during this period was Stourbridge, where several important companies produced the majority of the work associated with this revival. Although the vase included here is unsigned, it relates closely in technique and style to several pieces signed by Thomas Webb and Sons. The circumstances of its acquisition by the Fricks are unknown. It may have been bought or received as a gift with the other English cameo vase in the collection, because in early photographs of the reception room and library at Clayton the two are always displayed together.   E. P. D.

7.

7. Coffeepot (from a Five-piece Coffee Service), 1880-90

Maker: Whiting Manufacturing Company, North Attleboro, Massachusetts (1866-1926)
Silver, copper, ivory
H: Coffeepot: 7⅘ in. (19.7 cm.)
Stamped on bottom of all pieces: standing two-headed griffin with circled *W* all enclosed in a rectangle [Whiting trademark] *STERLING/412/P*

More than any other medium, American silver of the late nineteenth century shows the influence of Japanese crafts. After the display of Japanese objects at the Philadelphia Centennial Exposition of 1876, Americans developed a particular interest in Japanese metalwork, as exemplified by bronze vases found at Clayton (cat. no. 4). Even earlier, American silver designers had turned to these works as a new and refreshing source of inspiration for their designs.

Whiting Manufacturing Company is noted for its imaginative designs, particularly those in the Anglo-Japanese style produced in the 1880s and 1890s. The coffee and tea service at Clayton is a good example of this. The surface of each piece is hand hammered—a finishing technique developed by Tiffany & Co. around 1876 and called "martelé" by the French critics who saw the firm's display at the 1878 Paris Exposition. Applied onto the sur-

6.

face in silver and copper are oak leaves, berries, pine cones, and corn flowers, using a technique of mixed metal appliqué which Tiffany & Co. had developed in 1873. And, the form of each piece, while not Japanese per se, is Oriental in feeling. The charm of this service comes in part from the surprising use of American rather than Japanese naturalistic elements, as would have been typical of Anglo-Japanese silver.

It is not known when the Fricks purchased or were given this service, nor does it appear in any early photographs. However, it is stylistically in keeping with the furnishings they acquired in their first effort at decorating Clayton.   E. M. R.

8. *Covered Vase, 1887*

Maker: Derby Crown Porcelain Company Limited, Derby, England (c. 1750-1890, thereafter, Royal Crown Derby)

Porcelain, enameled and gilded

H: 12 in. (30.4 cm.)

Marked on vase and cover: printed overglaze in red, a crown over entwined double-D cipher; the cover also has the date device; the vase is further marked in red: *W. W. WATTLES & CO./PITTS-BURGH,* and painted in overglaze red *513/2594*

Purchased: W. W. Wattles & Co., Pittsburgh, Pennsylvania, c. 1887

Llewellynn Jewitt's influential volume *The Ceramic Art of Great Britain* (1883) served to highlight Britain's past successes in the ceramic arts and promote her industry. His assessment of the work produced by the Derby Crown Porcelain Company at the time was especially favorable:

The specialties [of Derby] are the vases, principally of Persian and Indianesque character, decorated in the richest styles with a profusion of raised gilt ornament and an elaborate coloring that is eminently effective. In this raised gold species of decoration, these works are markedly successful.... In whatever style, indeed, the decoration of these choice cabinet specimens is done there is a studied delicacy and beauty that are in keeping with the apparently fragile body of which they are composed. [New York: A. Worthington, 1883]

This vase, purchased around 1887 from W. W.

Wattles, a prominent Pittsburgh china and glass dealer, matches closely Jewitt's description of choice cabinet specimens, including the elaborate brilliant-yellow ground color, the rich profusion and studied delicacy of the raised gilt ornament, and the Persian character of the molded design around the neck and on the cover.

Porcelain had been made in Derby since about 1750, but the Derby Crown Porcelain Company was newly organized in 1876 by Edward Phillips, a Staffordshire potter, and his principal partner William Litherland, a Liverpool china and glass dealer. Guided by Richard Lunn, the art director, the new factory became well known for opulent decoration. In addition to cabinet pieces, the firm also produced special services naturalistically hand-painted with game, birds, or waterscapes. After January 1890, when Queen Victoria appointed the company as her porcelain manufacturer, it was called Royal Crown Derby.   E. P. D.

8.

9.

9. Armchair, 1892

Designer: Frederick J. Osterling, Pittsburgh,
 Pennsylvania (1865-1934)
Maker: A. Kimbel & Sons, New York, New York
 (1882-1925)
Mahogany, leather
H: 50¼ in. (127.2 cm.)
Unmarked
Purchased: A Kimbel & Sons, New York, New York,
 October 25, 1892

In October 1892, A. Kimbel & Sons, New York, billed Henry Clay Frick for a new suite of dining room furniture for Clayton, including "18 chairs, elaborately carved, covered with illuminated Cordovan leather" at $75 each, and "2 Armchairs to match," $110 each. The chairs were only part of the 1892 remodeling of the dining room, in which the room was enlarged and all furniture, fixtures,

woodwork, and hangings were designed and custom-made to achieve a cohesive effect. Such attempts to bring all decorating elements into harmony typified the most stylish houses of the last decades of the nineteenth century. In many cases, decorating firms planned and made the furnishings; at Clayton, however, it was Frederick Osterling (architect of the 1892 exterior remodeling) who developed plans for the woodwork in many of the rooms and for the complete redecoration of the dining room and the library.

Several of Osterling's watercolor sketches for the dining room were found in the attic at Clayton in 1986. A sketch of the east wall showing built-in cabinets, draperies, and decorative window transoms (see page 32), is very similar to the current scheme. While there is no sketch for a chair similar to the one pictured here, correspondence indicates that A. Kimbel & Sons worked from the architect's designs. We can therefore assume that Osterling designed the chairs.

The large arched fireplace in the dining room indicates Osterling's indebtedness to H. H. Richardson, who had designed the Allegheny Court House in 1888. Indeed, the chairs show Osterling's interest in the same design sources that inspired Richardson. The foliate swirl carving on the crest rail of the chairs has often been called "Richardsonian Romanesque," although here, with intervening interlaced elements it more closely resembles the models for Byzantine ornament shown in Owen Jones's *The Grammar of Ornament*, originally published in England in 1856 and widely circulated in America. In scale and form these chairs look backward to the baronial chairs of the baroque era; however, the naturalistic ornament heralds the Art Nouveau style.

As part of her initial preparation for opening the house to the public in 1953, Miss Helen Clay Frick asked interior decorator Scott Green of Joseph Horne Co., Pittsburgh, to have the dining room chairs reupholstered with "special hand tooled leather." According to Mr. Green, every attempt was made to duplicate the original, and the contract specified that the "old leather [was] to be removed from chairs carefully and returned to owner." So far, it has not been found.   E. M. R.

10. Andiron (One of a Pair), 1892

Designer: Attributed to Frederick J. Osterling
    (1882-1925)

Maker: A. Kimbel & Sons, New York, New York
    (1882-1941)

Nickel-plated brass, iron

H: 34½ in. (87.63 cm.)

Unmarked

Purchased: A. Kimbel & Sons, New York, New York,
    October 25, 1892

On October 25, 1892, A. Kimbel & Sons billed for over $13,000 of work in the dining room at Clayton including "1 pair Andirons, oxidized silver finish. 188.00." The firm, in operation from 1863 to 1882 as A. Kimbel and J. Cabus and thereafter as A. Kimbel & Sons, had long had a reputation for excellent decorating and furniture making. Indeed, on its letterhead, the company described itself as follows: "Upholsterers, Furniture Makers and Fresco Painters." A catalogue of photographs of the company's work dating from the 1870s through the 1890s (now in the library of the Cooper-Hewitt Museum, New York) shows that metal work was also part of its repertoire. Whether the firm con-

tracted out for metal furnishings or made them in its own factory is not known.

There are two documented examples of A. Kimbel & Sons' metal craftsmanship at Clayton: the iron-work grilles for arches in the second floor hall and these andirons. In each case the work was custom-designed to incorporate decorative motifs employed in other furnishings in the room and therefore to create the harmonious effect recommended as desirable by late-nineteenth-century decorating specialists.

In comparing the andirons with the dining room chairs, we can see the use of the same patterns. The acanthus swirl of the chair's crest rail is simplified, expanded, and used in the cap and base. The flaring chair rail finial is mirrored in the broadening upper part of the andiron. Finally, the twisting interlacing carving in the chair's crest rail is mimicked by the andiron's twisting upright and cross rail (cat. no. 9).

It is known from sketches that Frederick J. Osterling, architect of the 1892 remodeling of Clayton, drew up plans for the design and coordination of all furnishings in the dining room, including andirons. However, the one andiron sketch found at Clayton does not conform to these. While we suspect that Osterling's plans were followed in producing these andirons, in the absence of a working drawing we cannot know for certain (see photograph on page 33).   E. M. R.

10.

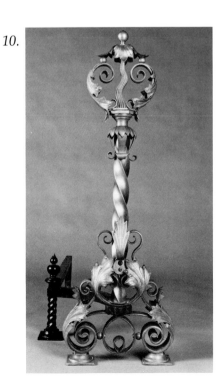

11. Covered Vase, 1889-1900

Modeler: James Hadley (1837-1903)

Maker: Worcester Royal Porcelain Company,
    Worcester, England (1862-present)

Porcelain, enameled and gilded

H: 18¼ in. (46.3 cm.)

Mark of the company printed in purple with Registry
    No. *137105,* shape number *1399* and initials *CR/A;*
    Hadley is intaglio molded on front shoulder

In ceramics, as in other media, the emergence of the Renaissance-revival style was tied closely to the proliferation of art histories published during the second half of the nineteenth century, first by German, and later, by English authors. Numerous

11.

volumes beginning with Jacob Burckhardt's *Die Kultur der Renaissance* (1860), and continuing beyond John Addington Symonds's seven volumes of *The Renaissance in Italy* (1875-1886), gave artists and designers an extensive vocabulary of masks, friezes, festoons, figures, and other ornaments to arrange and rearrange to evoke the grandeur and sumptuousness of the Renaissance.

In Worcester, the modeler James Hadley was the master of creating the Renaissance illusion, as shown in this covered vase with fluted neck and masks of lions and putti joined by festoons. The painting, executed by an unidentified Worcester artist, is classically studied and balanced, but rendered with Victorian color and flourish.

James Hadley worked as a modeler in Worcester's porcelain factory from the mid-1870s until he went out on his own in 1875. Even then most of his work for the next twenty years continued to be for the Worcester Royal Porcelain Company. Indeed, he was largely responsible for creating the high quality in design that is closely associated with Worcester because he produced so many of the important shapes.   E. P. D.

12. Two-handled Cup, 1893

Maker: Gorham Manufacturing Company, Providence, Rhode Island (1863-present)
Silver, colorless glass
H: 10 in. (24.9 cm.)
Stamped on bottom: lion, anchor, *G/51525/two joined circles/5 Pint*; scratched on: *TEX*
Monogrammed: *AHCF/Xmas 1895*
Purchased: probably, J. C. Grogan, Pittsburgh, Pennsylvania, June 18, 1895

It was usual in the late nineteenth century to find forms previously associated with purely sacred practices appropriated for secular, decorative uses. Altarpieces became sideboards and ecclesiastical vestments became piano scarfs. In this silver and glass two-handled cup we find a reinterpretation of the silver-mounted rock crystal reliquary of the Renaissance. The form, with cast Renaissance masks and gadrooned bottom of molded and engraved glass, is that of a presentation cup, and yet it appears in early Clayton photographs holding a bouquet of roses and carnations.

Dated by the Gorham mark for 1893, the cup represents the company's renewed interest in authentic-looking detail and increased attention to

12.

craftsmanship. A firm of great longevity and production capacity, Gorham is considered one of the most important silver-making firms of the late nineteenth and twentieth centuries. The firm's products were distributed widely and it seems that Henry Clay Frick purchased this cup from J. C. Grogan, Pittsburgh, in June 1895, paying $71.25. It was a Christmas gift to Mrs. Frick.   E. M. R.

13. Ewer, c. 1895

Maker: Coalport, Coalport, England (c. 1796-1925)
Porcelain, enameled and gilded
H: 10¼ in. (27.4 cm.)
Mark printed in green underglaze:
  ENGLAND/[crown]/*COALPORT*/*A.D. 1750*;
  painted in grey *V2562*

The porcelain factory at Coalport was established by John Rose around 1796 and was best known during the mid-nineteenth century for imitations of antique Sèvres, Meissen, and Chelsea porcelains. Although the factory's reputation declined between 1862 and 1885 when its ownership was in dispute, quality was resumed and some new styles and methods introduced when Thomas John Bott became art director in 1890 under the company's new owner Charles Clarke Bruff.

The application of raised colored enamel dots—a method known as ''jeweling''—was an old process in the English repertoire of ceramic decoration when it was introduced into Coalport's production in the early 1890s. Nonetheless, the factory's new work was of sufficient quality to arouse critical interest. In 1892, for example, the *Pottery Gazette* noted that Coalport's ''ornamentation is exceedingly rich, and is shown on a great variety of fancy shapes....The imitations of jewelled setting is [sic] very perfect, particularly the topaz and pearl.''

Elaborately jeweled examples were included in Coalport's display at the 1893 World's Columbian Exposition in Chicago and won a gold medal and much publicity. Such renown undoubtedly attracted the attention of Mr. and Mrs. Frick, who added to their collection of English porcelain cabinet pieces a jeweled basket that had been in Coalport's display at the 1893 Fair in addition to

this ewer with more satisfactory decoration executed in a similar fashion.

Like so many other examples in the Fricks' collection, the ewer is in the Renaissance-revival style with its classical shape, entwined snake handle, and jeweled mantel on the shoulder. The gilding and jeweling of pieces like this one were done by highly skilled gilders and enamelers who rarely signed their work.   E. P. D.

13.

14. Champagne Glass, 1880-1900

Maker: Unknown, Bohemia (now Czechoslovakia)
Colorless glass, engraved and gilded
H: 4¾ in. (12 cm.)
Unmarked
Monogrammed: *AHCF*

Although Clayton's sideboards and cupboards are filled with sets of beautifully cut or engraved glassware purchased for use in the dining room, the most impressive group is the Bohemian engraved and gilded table service bearing Mrs. Frick's monogram, a piece of which is included here. The skills of American glass cutters, particularly those in Pittsburgh, were well matched with those of their Anglo-Irish competitors during the late nineteenth century, but the desire of wealthy Americans for large, elaborately decorated table services could be answered only by the work of Continental craftsmen.

The diversification of forms available for a single glass table service had begun in the eighteenth century, but by the late nineteenth century as many as eleven different types of drinking vessels could be ordered for one place setting. In addition, these matched services could include fruit sets, finger bowls, wine ewers, and a variety of serving plates and dishes, as does the service at Clayton.

Like many other decorative objects at Clayton, this service evokes the Renaissance in the lavishness of the engraving and gilding, but especially in the attenuated shapes and the bosses on the hollow forms.   E. P. D.

14.

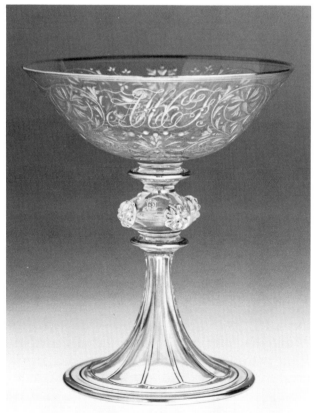

15.

15. Dessert Plate (from a Service of Twelve), 1899

Decorator: Samuel Alcock (born c.1846)

Maker: W. T. Copeland and Sons, Stoke-on-Trent, England (1867-1970, now Spode)

Porcelain, enameled and gilded

Diam: 9⁵/₁₆ in. (23.5 cm.)

Marked in green underglaze *COPELANDS CHINA/ ENGLAND*; printed in gold overglaze *Davis Collamore & Co., Ltd./FIFTH AVE & 37TH ST/NEW YORK*; signed *S. Alcock* in the decoration on each plate

Purchased: Davis Collamore & Co., Ltd., New York, December 19, 1899

On December 19, just in time for the Christmas celebration in 1899, Henry Clay Frick purchased two dessert services for twelve from Davis Collamore & Co., Ltd., a leading New York china and glass dealer. The first, and lesser, service was probably produced at Mintons because the invoice names Boullemiere, one of that manufacturer's decorators, as the artist. Frick paid $300 for the Minton service, which he had sent to a family friend. The second service, decorated by Samuel Alcock, he took home to Mrs. Frick. The price, $925, reflected Alcock's reputation in the ceramic arts.

Samuel Alcock was described in Llewellynn Jewitt's informative volume *The Ceramic Art of Great*

Britain (1883) as "a figure-painter of great power and excellence." Trained in the Royal Academy Schools, Alcock worked for W. T. Copeland from the 1880s until the early years of the twentieth century. As seen here, he painted figure studies in contemporary or classical dress in a muted poetic style on a white porcelain ground without detailed settings. Because he was the firm's premier painter, his work was presented in the most elaborate borders, which were prepared by Copeland's talented staff of ground-layers, pasteworkers, gilders, and enamelers.

Founded by Josiah Spode II in 1797, the firm made porcelain from the beginning as Spode, then as Copeland and Garrett, as W. T. Copeland and, after 1867, as W. T. Copeland and Sons. All of the companies that operated this factory were known for exceptional porcelain painting.   E. P. D.

16.

16. *Figural Sweetmeat Baskets (from a Dessert Table Service of Ten), 1891-1900*

Modeler: James Hadley (1837-1903)
Maker: Worcester Royal Porcelain Company, Worcester, England (1862-present)
Porcelain, enameled and gilded
H: (Male Figure) 8¼ in. (21 cm.)
Mark of the company printed overglaze in purple with Registry No. *60367* and shape number *1177; Hadley* is intaglio molded on figure of seated boy with basket.

James Hadley's work for Worcester was so varied that he was known for his designs in the Japanese and Victorian aesthetic tastes as well as for his Renaissance-revival vases (see cat. no. 11). This group of figures is rendered in the attitudes and dress of the popular Victorian illustrator Kate Greenaway.

These engaging children and adolescents display baskets that would have carried small sweets for dessert. As figures serving the diners, they follow a tradition that began more than a century earlier in which the human form was frozen in animated miniature to entertain and serve at table. The subjects are depicted both as children and as courting adolescents.   E. P. D.

17. *Vase, 1900*

Decorator: Frederick Sturgis Laurence (active at Rookwood 1895-1903)
Maker: Rookwood Pottery Company, Cincinnati, Ohio (1880-1960)
Earthenware, colored slips
H: 14½ in. (39.9 cm.)
Marked on bottom: impressed *RP* monogram with fourteen flames over *821/A*; incised *CHIEF 'GOOSE,'/SIOUX/SL*
Purchased: Hamilton & Clark, Pittsburgh, Pennsylvania, December 11, 1901

The three examples at Clayton of the Rookwood Pottery Company's sturdy earthenware stand in marked contrast to the brightly colored and gilded English porcelains that predominated in the Fricks' decorative scheme. Decorated in a somber palette of browns, oranges, and greens they include this vase, a loving cup depicting the actor Joseph Jefferson as "Caleb Plummer," also by Laurence, and a vase with poppies decorated by Matt Daley.

Founded in 1880 as a quasi-amateur operation by prominent Cincinnati socialite Maria Longworth Nichols, the Rookwood Pottery was an outgrowth of her avid interest in china painting. When her friend William Watts Taylor took charge in 1883, he standardized production by employing academy-trained artists to execute decorations in the limited color and subject ranges that had proven to be the most saleable. He promoted the collecting of Rookwood as an American art form by having each piece carefully dated and signed with that company's mark and the artist's cypher. Flowers, animals, children, characters from

17.

literature and the theater were popular subjects for Rookwood's vases; and heads of Indians were more numerous in the pottery's repertoire after 1895, when art photographers like Edward Curtis began publishing Indian portraits. At this time, Rookwood's objective in portraiture was to produce vases that looked like Old Master paintings.

The promotion of Rookwood pottery as art may have prompted Mrs. Frick's purchase of this vase depicting Chief Goose, a Sioux Indian. The vase was bought for $75.00 from Hamilton & Clark, Pittsburgh china and glass dealers. The invoice notes that it had been shown at the Pan-American Exposition at Buffalo, New York, during the summer of 1901, a world's fair at which Rookwood had won a Gold Medal for its display. A reporter for *Keramic Studio*, November, 1901, described the Pottery's Pan-American exhibit as "The Mecca of all lovers of decoration in keramics.... The Standard

ware, as it is called, is still as good as ever, and the Indian heads which started the present craze for things Indian, are as effective as ever." The reporter continued, "We have a right to feel proud of this American achievement in pottery," a sentiment echoed by Helen Clay Frick in an explanatory note found in another example of Rookwood earthenware at Clayton. E. P. D.

18. *Loving Cup, 1893*

Maker: Dominick & Haff, Inc., New York, New York and Newark, New Jersey (1889-1928)
Silver
H: 9⅝ in. (23.9 cm.)
Marked on bottom: incised rectangle enclosing *925*, connected to empty circle, connected to triangle enclosing *1893/STERLING 255/6½ pts*
Monogrammed: *AHCF Xmas 1895*
Anonymous loan

Adelaide Frick received several gifts of silver for Christmas 1895, including this loving cup and a silver and glass cup (cat. no. 12). Although similar in size and general form and of the same date, the two are stylistically quite dissimilar. The design of the loving cup, executed in the Art Nouveau style, albeit with rococo motifs, looks forward to the twentieth century. The silver and glass cup, on the other hand, is Renaissance-revival in style, carrying on the tradition of historical revival that had dominated design during the last half of the nineteenth century. In tune with the eclecticism of the period, both pieces were displayed in a room decorated in yet a third style, the Louis XV reception room.

This three-handled cup with flared mouth is ornamented with repoussé and chased foliate decoration, including three cartouches and groupings of sprigs and berries. In contrast to the martelé finish often found on American Art Nouveau silver, the polished and faintly ribbed surface of this cup accentuates the pleasing fluidity of the swirling ornament. Although little has been written about Dominick & Haff, the makers of this cup, its evident quality suggests that they merit further consideration.

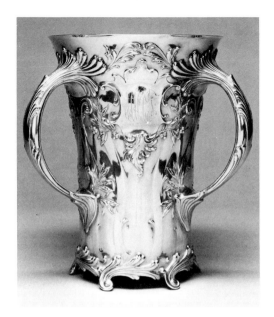

18.

While the loving cup has traditionally been considered a presentation piece, at Clayton it was put to more practical uses. In a dining room photograph taken around 1900 it sits near the end of a set table holding a bottle of wine. In a reception room photograph from around the same time, it rests on a small table surrounded by goblets. A glass liner insert is visible, suggesting that the loving cup may have been used for ice, or again as a wine cooler.   E. M. R.

19. Tea Set, 1892

Maker: A. I. Kuzmichev, Moscow, Russia (1856-1917)
Silver-gilt, enamels
H: (Tea Pot) 5½ in. (13.9 cm.)
Marked on bottom of tray: *A.A.* over *1892/88/ MADE FOR TIFFANY & Co./A.K.*
Monogrammed: *AHCF*
Purchased: Tiffany & Co., New York, New York, December 15, 1894

Henry Clay Frick purchased this silver-gilt and enameled Russian tea set from Tiffany & Co., New York, in 1894 for $500. Tiffany's, retailer of fine wares from around the world, seems to have been a favorite stop for the Fricks when in New York. Record of their first purchase from this store dates from 1881, and Tiffany's remained a frequent source for their purchases of decorative accessories from then on.

This tea set was part of a new line of silver enamelware made especially for Tiffany's by the prestigious Moscow firm of A. I. Kuzmichev, which, along with other Russian firms, revived the seventeenth-century Russian craft of enameling. The first Tiffany advertisement for Russian enamels appeared in its *Blue Book* for 1893, only a

19.

year before this purchase. The stamped mark represents the following: ''A.A.'' stands for ''Made for Tiffany & Co.,'' and ''1892'' the year; ''88'' is the Russian silver quality mark, and ''A.K.'' stands for the manufacturer.

Decorated with vibrant enamels of dark blue, turquoise, purple, white, and red fitted between filigree in a cloisonné technique, this tea set seems a very special purchase. Since it was acquired on December 15, the day before Mrs. Frick's birthday, and each piece is engraved with her monogram, it may well be that this was a birthday gift from her husband. The set is unique in the Fricks' collection at Clayton, which includes no more than a handful of enameled objects and no other examples of Russian craftsmanship.   E. M. R.

20. Vase, c. 1899-1905

Maker: Doulton and Company, Burslem, England
   (1882-present; at Lambeth since 1815)
Porcelain, enameled and gilded
H: 18¼ in. (46.6 cm.)
Marked with underglaze in green twice: a crown
   above the lobed device for *DOULTON.*
   BURSLEM above *ENGLAND*; and printed in red
   overglaze *LACTOLIAN/WARE*

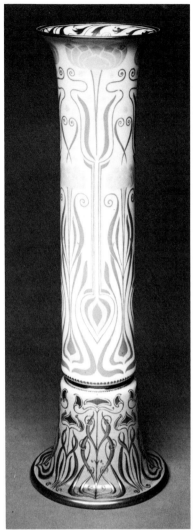

20.

Few pieces in the collection of ceramics at Clayton could be described as being as avant-garde as the Doulton Lactolian Ware vase shown here, an English homage to the patterned abstract designs developed in Glasgow, Vienna, and Berlin at the turn of the twentieth century. Despite its contrast to the Renaissance-style and Victorian wares that predominate in Clayton's collection, however, this vase was always kept in the library, which seems to have housed ceramics that especially interested the Frick family.

Lactolian Ware characterized by pâte-sur-pâte (a form of relief decoration achieved by the application of slips) was developed at Doulton by art director John Slater and artist William G. Hodkinson. Although it was introduced in 1900 at the same Paris Exposition that featured French Art Nouveau, it did not become popular and was discontinued soon after.

Founded as Doulton and Watts at Lambeth in 1815, Doulton's potteries were well-known for their high-grade sanitary, industrial, and architectural ceramics when the firm began to experiment with art wares in the late 1860s at the urging of John Sparkes, principal of the Lambeth School of Art. These early art wares were so well received at international exhibitions in 1867 and 1871 that Henry Doulton gradually expanded the program, and by 1882 had bought full interest in the Burslem earthenware firm of Pinder Bourne and Company. Under art directors John Slater and, after 1914, Charles J. Noke, the Burslem works became a leading art pottery.   E. P. D.

21. Dresser Set, 1904

Maker: Tiffany & Co., New York, New York
  (1853-present)
Silver, enamel, silver gilt, down, silk
H: (Puff Box) 6¼ in. (15.7 cm.)
Marked on bottom of puff box: *TIFFANY &*
  CO./16112 MAKERS 6850/STERLING SILVER/
  925-100/C
Monogrammed: *AHCF*
Purchased: Tiffany & Co., New York, New York,
  October 27, 1904

On October 27, 1904, the year before the family's move to New York, Henry Clay Frick purchased a fourteen-piece dresser set from Tiffany & Co. and had it monogrammed for his wife. Including a puff box with silver-topped puff, mirror, three glass and silver toilet bottles, pin box, tray, two salve boxes, shoehorn, button hook, shell and silver comb, jewel box, and ivory and silver mirror, the set cost $2,820. While matching dresser sets had been made in England as early as the seventeenth century, they did not appear in America until the nineteenth century, when they soared in popularity.

There are many silver dresser sets in Clayton's collections. Photographs of the house taken around 1900 show silver implements on nearly every dresser and dressing table. This dresser set is of interest, however, because it departs stylistically from the other sets that are, by and large, rococo in feeling. The forms of this set generally suggest the covered cups and carved cassone of the Renaissance. However, the ornament—applied knights in armor and crowns and shields with heraldic crests—seems drawn from the lore of European aristocracy. As such, the dresser set is more in keeping with the Fricks' taste after they moved to the "Medicean" Vanderbilt house they rented in New York than when they lived at Clayton.   E. M. R.

22. Desk Set (Seven of Fourteen Pieces), c.1900-1910

Maker: Unknown, probably American
Brass, silver
H: (Rack) 9⅗ in. (19.1 cm.)
Marked: Brass and Silver
Monogrammed: *HCF*

This desk set is undocumented as to manufacturer, place, and date of purchase, or use. Nonetheless, it is so charming that it merited inclusion in this catalogue.

The life of the mind was of particular importance to Americans of means in the late nineteenth century. Similarly, expression of an interest in learning and study were fundamental to home furnishing. The library, with its displays of books, artifacts of historical or cultural significance, roomy tables, and comfortable reading chairs became a

21.

22.

center of family life. This Victorian inclination toward study and specialization made multi-part desk sets of enormous proportion highly popular in the late nineteenth century. Sets like the one pictured here frequently included a stationary rack, pen bottle, bill file, blotter, stamp box, tape measure, letter opener, ink eraser, sealing wax set, sealing wax ladle, seal, candlestick, moistener, scissors, inkstand, twine holder, check cutter, match vase, calendar, thermometer, blotter corners, and pens.

Most of the desk sets made between the 1890s and 1920s were intended for men, and have a distinctly masculine quality. This is not the case with the set pictured here. Executed in textured brass with silver edging showing the rolls and flourishes of the Art Nouveau style, this set seems, particularly in contrast to other things owned by Henry Clay Frick, quite feminine in character. This suggests that the monogram may stand for Helen, rather than Henry, Clay Frick. Probably made after 1900, it would have been a most suitable accoutrement for the desk of a young woman with a keen interest in art and literature.   E. M. R.

23. *Music Cabinet, c.1906*

Maker: Unknown, possibly English
White holly, burl walnut, mahogany, pine,
    painted panels
H: 57⅝ in. (146.2 cm.)
Unmarked
Purchased: Cottier Galleries, New York, New York,
    April 14, 1906

This music cabinet bears considerable resemblance in scale, decoration, and configuration to cabinets designed by English Pre-Raphaelite artists of the 1860s. Several features, however, betray a date of manufacture some forty years later. While Pre-Raphaelite artists attempted to recapture the spirit of the Middle Ages, this music cabinet relies on classical models. The panels show draped Grecian figures painted to suggest crazing so as to create an antique effect. The refinement of the burl walnut veneer and painted flower and frond borders on the case and legs stands in sharp con-

trast to the deliberately rustic carpentry of the earlier cabinets.

On April 14, 1906, Henry Clay Frick and his wife purchased the music cabinet from Cottier Galleries, New York, for $2,200 for their new residence at 640 Fifth Avenue. Cottier Galleries was the retail division of Cottier and Company, a prestigious decorating firm with offices in London, New York, Sydney, and Melbourne, begun by Scotsman Daniel Cottier (1838-1891). The New York branch, opened in 1873, was employed by the Fricks for the decoration of four of their residences: their apartment at Sherry's, New York (1902); a redecoration of Clayton (1903-4); 640 Fifth Avenue (1906); and Eagle Rock in Massachusetts (1906). While Cottier and Company may have made this cabinet, it appears that Cottier Galleries sold mainly imported and antique furnishings. The Fricks' other purchases from the store included an

23.

"antique Chinese Rug," a "Persian Embroidery," "4 Old Queen Anne Chairs," and an "Antique Gilt Frame." Such goods were increasingly prized after the turn of the century.

In 1984, the cabinet still contained a yellowed scroll describing scenes from the myth of Orpheus painted on the panels. Orpheus, a Greek demigod, had musical abilities so powerful that he was able to charm everything inanimate and living, mortal and immortal. The front panels show Orpheus's journey to the underworld to plead for the return of his wife Eurydice.

Inside are fifteen drawers of white holly. Centered on the front of each drawer are empty ovals on which were to have been painted the "name of composer or class of music in drawer." On the original purchase annotation F. V. Hart is named as the decorator of the "trays," presumably the interior drawers. No artist is listed for the painted panels, and no maker given for the case.

This was one of the few pieces of furniture the Fricks moved from 640 Fifth Avenue to their new house at 1 East 70th Street in 1914. In 1932, after Mrs. Frick's death, the cabinet was brought to the parlor at Clayton, where it remains.   E. M. R.

24. Writing Table (Bureau-plat), c.1774

Maker: Attributed to Martin Carlin, Paris, France (active 1766-85)

H: 30⅜ in. (77.1 cm.); W: 23⅝ in. (60.0 cm.); L: 50⅝ in. (128.5 cm.)

Tulipwood, oak, porcelain, gilt bronze, leather

Unmarked case. Plaques nearly all painted with blue interlacing *L's*, some enclosing the letter *V* and surmounted by a comma.

Provenance: J. Pierpont Morgan Collection; purchased from Duveen Brothers, New York, New York, July 6, 1915

Martin Carlin is particularly noted for the elegance of his furniture, derived from well-balanced proportions, refined workmanship, and an assiduous use of plaques of Sèvres porcelain. A writing table marked by Carlin, owned by James A. de Rothschild at Waddesdon Manor, bears a marked resemblance to the writing table at Clayton. It is this similarity, as well as correspondences to other

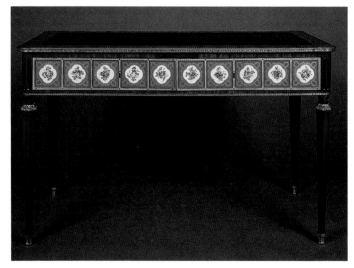

24.

works that bear Carlin's stamp, that prompts this attribution.

Little is known about the life of Martin Carlin. Born in the German state of Baden, he first appears in Parisian records in 1759, when he was named in a lawsuit. Presumably he was by then already advanced in his career, for he became a *maître-ébéniste* (master cabinet maker) on July 30, 1766. While it seems unlikely that he was ever officially appointed by the Court, it is known that he completed commissions for members of the royal family. Carlin died in Paris in March 1785.

The table is a classic example of the Louis XVI period, displaying tapered hexagonal legs and a rectangular table top covered with now faded green leather, cast gilt bronze mounts, and veneered exotic wood. Recessed writing panels on either side are covered in vibrant green leather, which, having remained unexposed to light, still matches the green ground of the twenty-eight plaques that surround the case.

The soft-paste porcelain plaques with green ground, polychrome flowers, and gilt decoration nearly all bear the crossed *L's* of the Sèvres factory, a mark used since 1753, when the king became the principal shareholder. All plaques removed for inspection appear to be original to the writing table, however, they are not marked identically. Some are marked with the date letter *V* for the year 1774 and by a comma, which is the mark attributed to Charles-Louis Mereau (1756-1779, known as Mereau jeune) painter of flowers and ornament.

It is entirely possible that the plaques are of different dates, ranging from 1774 up to the time the table was constructed.

Formerly in the possession of J. Pierpont Morgan, the table was part of the large collection of eighteenth-century French furniture loaned by the Morgan estate to the Metropolitan Museum of Art. Much of that collection was bought by Henry Clay Frick through Duveen Brothers for his newly built home in New York. However, this table, purchased on July 6, 1915, for $35,000, was for the Fricks' summer house in Prides Crossing and appears in a photograph of the music room there (see page 35). It was brought to Clayton in 1955 with other pieces of eighteenth-century French furniture and the collection of Chinese miniature porcelains also from Prides Crossing. At that time, in preparation for opening Clayton to the public, Miss Frick refurnished the reception room, which had stood empty for many years.   E. M. R.

25. *Candlestick (One of Four) with Bobeche, 1738*

Maker: Paul Crespin, London, England (1694-1770)
Silver
H: 10 in. (25.4 cm.)
Stamped on base: standing lion, *P.C.* over a star, leopard's head crown, *C/B* over *A*F/No. 1/30 = 18*; bobeche is unmarked
Provenance: Sir Sidney Greville Collection; purchased from Elsie de Wolfe, New York, New York, October 14, 1914
Anonymous loan

The rococo style first appeared in English silver in the early 1720s. It was spread by English craftsmen, who borrowed freely from French prints and pattern books that arrived in London in the 1730s. Engravings by Juste Aurele Meissonier, the great French silversmith, were especially influential. Interpretations of the rococo by the Huguenot craftsmen who had fled to London from France following the revocation of the Edict of Nantes in 1685 epitomized the style. Paul de Lamerie is the most celebrated of these French Protestant silversmiths, however, the somewhat younger Paul Crespin, maker of these candlesticks, is almost as well known.

Born in 1694 in Giles, Westminster, Paul Crespin was apprenticed at the age of nineteen. Although he never became a Freeman of the Goldsmiths' Company, his work brings a vitality to rococo silver often lacking in French work. The four candlesticks at Clayton, made in 1738, represent the fully developed English rococo style, making abundant use of shell forms, acanthus leaves, and C-scrolls in an asymmetrical composition. They are cast in solid silver, apparently by the traditional French method of lost wax or *cire perdue*.

The candlesticks are fully stamped with the marks of London assay office indicating silver content and year. The mark *B* over *A * F* was the standard form of monogramming for marrying couples, the top initial representing the surname and the lower initials representing the two first names. The small deer head engraved in one of three cartouches may have been the family insignia, or a decorative element copied from one of the many books on cartouches available at the time.

The flower-form bobeches are not marked, an omission that raises some questions as to their authenticity given the carefulness of English assay offices in the eighteenth century. There is evidence

25.

of later alterations to the bobeches, suggesting either that the marks were obscured at that time or that they were later, adapted additions.

Henry Clay Frick purchased all four candlesticks from decorator Elsie de Wolfe in October 1914 for $1,800 for use in the breakfast room at 1 East 70th Street. Presumably, they were moved to Clayton following Mrs. Frick's death in 1931. E. M. R.

26. *Plate (from a Service of Twenty-four), 1911*

Decorator: Alboine Birks (1861-1941)

Maker: Mintons Limited, Stoke-on-Trent, England (1796-1968)

Porcelain, enameled and gilded

Diam: 10$\frac{5}{16}$ in. (25.7 cm.)

Mark on bottom printed overglaze in purple includes a crown over a globe with *MINTONS*, all above *ENGLAND* and the retailer's identification: *Davis Collamore & Co. Ltd./FIFTH AVE & 48TH ST/ NEW YORK*; impressed in paste on bottom *MINTONS* and three factory symbols; signed on the front in the demi-lunes *ABirks*

Purchased: Davis Collamore & Co. Ltd., New York, New York, July 29, 1911

Mintons was especially famous during the late nineteenth century for its pâte-sur-pâte decoration, made in imitation of classical stone and glass cameos. In this method, delicate images were created laboriously by applying many layers of porcelain paste against a contrasting background. The undisputed master of this art was Louis Marc Solon (1835-1913), who introduced the pâte-sur-pâte technique to Mintons upon his arrival from France around 1870, and over the years trained a small group of talented and devoted artists in his studio. Alboine Birks, the decorator of this plate, was among them. Solon's studio was organized in the manner of the Renaissance, with Solon developing the figures and the apprentices responsible for routine decoration. Eventually, Birks and the others became proficient at figures too, producing important pieces for displays of the firm's wares at international exhibitions.

For production work like the plate shown here, however, molds were employed for establishing the body of the decoration, while details and refinements were added by the pâte-sur-pâte method. This practice allowed for faster production with a certain amount of standardization from plate to plate and also included enough participation by the artist to justify signing the work.

Even with the use of this production short-cut, a great amount of highly skilled artistry went into the making of this plate, one of fourteen that survive from a service of twenty-four. Although the service was not purchased for use in Clayton's dining room, its presence in the collection provides an index of how the Frick family's decorating preferences changed after the turn of the century to the chaste neoclassical taste shown in subsequent houses. At the same time, a plate like this, with its pâte-sur-pâte demi-lunes and raised gold paste decoration, shows that the Fricks never compromised their desire to see great skill lavished on an object that served an otherwise mundane purpose. E. P. D.

26.

27. Ewers, 1767

Maker: Pierre de Gouthière, Paris, France
  (1732-1813/14)
Gilt bronze
H: 11¼ in. (28.13 cm.)
Marked: *Fait Par Gouthière Ciseleur-Doreur/
  Du Roy Quay Pelletier 1767*
Provenance: Lord Hastings; J. Pierpont Morgan
  Collection; purchased from Duveen Brothers,
  New York, New York, May 27, 1916

Pierre de Gouthière was the most celebrated *ciseleur* (chaser) of his day. Born the son of a saddle-maker at Bar-sur-Aube, he is believed to have served an apprenticeship at Troyes. He moved to Paris in 1758 to work under François Ceriset, a master gilder, and in the same year married Ceriset's widow. Through this union he acquired

27.

Ceriset's shop, *La Boucle d'Or* (The Gold Buckle). It was thought that he did not execute any commissions for the Court until 1769; however, the inscription of 1767 on these ewers suggests a somewhat earlier affiliation. He continued to work for French nobility until 1777, but his financial rewards did not match his renown, since his clients repeatedly delayed payment. He declared bankruptcy in 1788, suffered further losses during the French Revolution, and died in poverty.

According to Pierre Verlet in *Les Bronzes Dorés Francais du XVIIIᵉ Siècle,* in which the ewers were published, they are among the earliest known works by the artist. As Verlet points out, in these ewers one can already see Gouthière's taste for vines, fauns, water nymphs, and rams' heads. The signature may be translated *Made by Gouthière chaser-gilder for the King, Wharf Pelletier 1767.*

On May 27, 1916, Henry Clay Frick purchased the ewers through Duveen Brothers for his home in Prides Crossing, Massachusetts. They had come from the estate of Frick's friend and business associate, J. Pierpont Morgan. Frick made many purchases from the Morgan estate through Duveen, including the canvases by Jean-Honoré Fragonard that he installed at 1 East 70th Street. At the time of Miss Frick's death, the ewers were displayed in the reception room and were presumably brought there from the Fricks' summer home at Prides Crossing in the 1950s, when Miss Frick refurnished the room with eighteenth-century French antiques owned by her parents. E. M. R.

The Clothing Collection at Clayton

In nothing are character and perception so insensibly but inevitably displayed as in dress and taste in dress. Dress is the second self—a dumb self, yet a most eloquent expositor of the person. Dress bears the same relation to the body as speech does to the brain, and therefore dress may be called the speech of the body. [Mary Eliza Haweis, The Art of Beauty, *1878]*

Comprising some 3,000 items of clothing and accessories from 1881-1930, the collection at Clayton offers yet another perspective on the attitudes and taste of the Frick family, particularly those of Mrs. Frick. While the collection also includes men's and children's clothing, it is especially strong in the clothing, underpinnings, hats, gloves, and shoes purchased and used by Mrs. Frick.

The collection includes examples of the silhouettes characteristic of each of the five decades of Mrs. Frick's married life. As might be expected, the clothing she saved tended to be the ensembles she wore on formal occasions. Made of the finest materials and ornamented with exquisite trim, Mrs. Frick's clothes were created by Pittsburgh dressmakers as well as by makers in New York, Paris, and London. Identification of the maker is often difficult because of a conspicuous absence of labels.

The Parisian houses Mrs. Frick is known to have patronized were Worth, Callot Soeurs, and Beer. Gustav Beer was a German designer who maintained an atelier in the Place Vendôme from 1905 until 1914 and was best known for elaborate evening clothes and lingerie. The description of his work as "conservative elegance for conservative patrons" fits Mrs. Frick's wardrobe in general, because even when she bought from other designers, she tended to choose their more conservative creations.

Invoices for yard goods and the presence of considerable amounts of trim in the collection suggest

Mrs. Frick in a picture hat with ostrich plumes, 1905. Large hats in this style balanced the "S-curve," or mono-bosom silhouette typical of this period.

that Mrs. Frick employed dressmakers, presumably local, to make some of her clothing. It would definitely be a mistake to assume that she bought all of her dresses, hats, and gowns from well-known designers.

Mrs. Frick's underpinnings reveal her love of lace and handwork. Consisting of petticoats, drawers, corset covers, and night dresses, they are made of the finest lawn and batiste, almost always

embroidered with her monogram and embellished with magnificent handmade lace, cut work, faggoting, embroidery, and pin-tucked flounces.

The collection of Mrs. Frick's shoes is small but of high quality and in exceptional condition. Made of leather or silk dyed to match particular gowns, the shoes are chiefly from the 1910s and 1920s.

Adelaide Howard Childs Frick wore this evening ensemble or "court dress" to a reception given at the White House by President Theodore Roosevelt. It was designed by Gustav Beer, owner of a design house in the Place Vendôme, Paris, from 1905 to 1914.

The silhouette of this bodice and skirt is typical of the early Edwardian period when, with the aid of a corset or sometimes a surgical procedure involving the removal of the bottom ribs, the female body was forced into a violent "S-curve." The bosom was thrust forward and was balanced "by the hips at the back" (the delicate term for the posterior).

The lace bodice is appliquéd with large, soft, cabbage-shaped rosettes made of gold tissue ribbon know as choux. These are embellished with embroidery of heavy gold metallic thread worked into a design of flowers, vines, and leaves. The sash on the bodice is ivory silk satin.

The ivory, silk velvet skirt has a front center panel of Brussels needlepoint lace which has been appliquéd with waves (known as galloons) of gold tissue ribbon. The velvet forming the skirt and train is appliquéd with choux and heavy gold embroidery, repeating the rosette and floral motifs found on the bodice. In addition there are several large medallions executed in heavy gold thread, worked in a pattern of webs, crosshatching, and swirls. Both the bodice and skirt are lined with silk taffeta and the train has an accordion-pleated balayeuse, or "dust ruffle," which has been edged in lace.

We can see from what survives of Mrs. Frick's clothing that white and ivory were favorite color choices for her evening gowns, and each of these gowns, almost without exception, has some lace on its bodice.

Beer was one of Mrs. Frick's favorite designers. Not only does his label appear more frequently than any other designer's label in the collection, but his is also the earliest "name" in the collection.

There is also an extensive assemblage of plumes and other hat trimmings. Sadly, few hats survive, for perhaps like many an indulgent grandmother, Mrs. Frick allowed her grandchildren to play "dress-up" with her bonnets and large picture hats. How well Mrs. Frick wore the elaborate hats of the pre-World War I decade can be seen from the photograph reproduced on page 59.

The collection includes only a few items of clothing that belonged to Helen Clay Frick. An evening gown, a yachting suit designed by Gustav Beer, and some side-saddle habits are all that we possess of this intellectual and unmaterialistic lady's wardrobe. While she conscientiously preserved all of the clothes that her mother had saved, she cared little for her own.

The items of clothing from Mr. Frick's wardrobe are primarily suits—black for most of the year and white for summer—and dress shirts, as well as undergarments and a few umbrellas, walking sticks, and hats. The Charvet silk-and-wool undergarments all bear ornate monograms and discreetly reveal the Parisian haberdasher's name in the weave of the fabric. Many of Mr. Frick's neckties also came from the house of Charvet.

The children's clothing at Clayton consists primarily of little girl's dresses made between 1883 and 1895, along with bonnets and shoes that suggest the doll-like quality of late-nineteenth-century children's clothes.

Above all, it is Adelaide Howard Childs Frick who speaks to us through this collection. Her clothes and those she chose for her children show the same concern for quality and restraint that characterized the household furnishings and decorations at Clayton. Showing signs of wear, hers are not the clothes of a self-indulgent woman quick to throw away last season's favorite dress. Nowhere is Mrs. Frick's taste for conservative elegance more evident than in the "court dress" pictured here. It was designed by Gustav Beer, and she wore it to the White House during the presidency of Theodore Roosevelt (1901-1908).

Louise F. Wells

"May be a little too enthusiastic about pictures"
Henry Clay Frick, the Young Collector

In November 1912, two years before Henry Clay Frick moved into the New York residence that would become The Frick Collection, his art collection was so renowned that a reviewer in *Connoisseur* magazine could write:

It is a very easy thing, given the money, to form an extensive collection of good examples of Old Masters, but it is quite another matter, even with unlimited resources, to form one which shall consist exclusively of great and famous pictures. By the exercise of an exacting and discriminating taste, Mr. Frick has succeeded in forming a collection, small as to numbers, but unrivalled in importance.

This is quite a statement considering that Frick had not yet purchased such masterpieces as Bellini's *St. Francis in Ecstasy,* Titian's *Portrait of a Man in a Red Cap,* and Fragonard's *The Progress of Love* series. As exceptional as was his collection in 1912, it was only half the world-famous collection ultimately assembled by Frick.

Frick's success in the uncertain world of art collecting is all the more remarkable because he neither grew up surrounded by art treasures nor received any formal education in art history or connoisseurship. Moreover, he never relied totally on the advice of his dealers; from the time he was a young man, Frick made his own art selections at whatever level he could afford. Although much has been written about his acquisition of great master paintings, little has been published about his earliest collecting in Pittsburgh. Fortunately, enough remains in old records and existing works of art at Clayton to piece together a reasonably accurate picture of the beginnings of Frick's collecting and of his early taste in art.

Exactly what art the young Mr. Frick purchased for himself while in his twenties is unknown, but that he did collect is certain. One telling remark exists in a report written about the twenty-two-year-old entrepreneur in 1871, when he asked for a loan from the Pittsburgh bank of T. Mellon & Sons. The report read:

Lands good, ovens well built; manager on job all day, keeps books evenings, may be a little too enthusiastic about pictures but not enough to hurt; knows his business down to the ground; advise making the loan.

Good advice to be sure, for by the end of the decade Frick was a millionaire and his years of serious collecting had begun.

The earliest surviving record of an art purchase follows by one month Frick's move into Pittsburgh and the Monongahela House, a fashionable downtown hotel. On February 12, 1881, he purchased "1 painting Hetzel" for $260 from S. Boyd & Company of Pittsburgh. This is certainly the *Landscape with River* painted by George Hetzel in 1880 (cat. no. 29). Hetzel, a nationally known artist, was one of several prominent Pittsburgh painters including John W. Beatty, A. Bryan Wall, and Joseph R. Woodwell, whom Frick would patronize throughout his years in the city. The Hetzel landscape is probably the painting Frick paid J. J. Gillespie & Company two dollars to hang on March 22, 1881. Gillespie's, a prominent Pittsburgh art gallery, served as the meeting place for many of the city's most talented artists at the time.

A number of art purchases followed the Hetzel in rapid succession as Frick continued to decorate the walls of his new apartment. On March 19, 1881, he bought "1 Genuine Bronze figure" from Grogan & Merz of Pittsburgh. Less than a week later, on March 24, he purchased from the New York dealer William Schaus an oil painting entitled

The reception room at Clayton hung with paintings of the Barbizon School, c.1900.

Une Révélation by Luis Jiménez y Aranda, together with two untitled watercolors by Eugène Cicéri, a watercolor by Madeleine Lemaire entitled *Expectation,* and a watercolor by Emil Adam entitled *A Conversation: Interior in Versailles.* Two days later, on March 26, Frick was back again at Schaus to pick out three more watercolors: *On the Oise* by C.-F.-A. de Mesgrigny, *In the Park at Fontainbleau* by J.-B.-G. Gassies, and *The Musician* by Louis Leloir. On March 31, Frick paid Gillespie's for ''2 men 2 days'' to ''hang pictures.''

Of the nine works of art purchased on this spree, Clayton still possesses the Jiménez painting and four of the watercolors by Cicéri, Lemaire, Adam, and de Mesgrigny. Together they exhibit enough

stylistic similarity to make possible some observations about Frick's early artistic preferences. All of these artists were late-nineteenth-century European painters working in a very traditional vein. The genre scenes by the first three artists are typically anecdotal. In the Jiménez—purchased with the title *A Revelation*—an elegantly dressed young woman gazes at a statue of a male nude as her mother looks disapproving and tries to move her along. The painting is called *In the Louvre* in the Frick family records. The Lemaire watercolor depicts a fashionably dressed young woman standing at the window of a well-appointed room. The scene takes on additional meaning when given the title *Expectation.* The Adam drawing likewise suggests a narrative with its eighteenth-century couple conversing in a richly decorated Versailles salon. All three works are very detailed, with colors and textures delineated with small, careful strokes. Frick's first choices, then, were all by academically trained, traditional artists.

The same is true for the landscapes by Cicéri and de Mesgrigny, which are similar to each other in composition and handling. Each depicts a quiet view of the French countryside with tall trees reflected in still water. There is little in the forms and careful brushwork to suggest even a casual awareness of the stylistic revolution being wrought by the Impressionists in landscape painting.

In the earliest photographs of Clayton, the Adam, de Mesgrigny, and Lemaire watercolors— all bought on the same New York trip two decades earlier—are seen hanging in Mr. Frick's bedroom. These works remained in Frick's collection at Clayton, even though he later traded or sold a great many of the art purchases from the late 1880s and 1890s. This suggests that Frick had a sentimental attachment to these earliest selections.

In 1881, Frick also began to purchase two series of books on French art and Old Master art. His self-education in art history was clearly under way.

Although Frick bought a few other inexpensive, untitled pastels and prints in 1881, his next significant acquisition was not until November 27, 1882, two months before he and Mrs. Frick moved into Clayton. At that time he purchased directly from the artist George Hetzel a painting entitled *Fruit*. Two days before the Clayton move on January 29, 1883, Frick bought from Gillespie's another painting of fruit, this time by A. Bryan Wall. Wall's father, Alfred S. Wall, was an artist who worked for Gillespie's and took over the art gallery in 1886 when Gillespie died. Both father and son were members with Hetzel of the "Scalp Level" artists, who painted landscapes of the mountains located east of Pittsburgh.

In December of 1883, Frick again purchased a painting from A. Bryan Wall: a large portrait of Frick's wife Adelaide and her sister Martha. Shortly thereafter, Frick must have commissioned a portrait of his one-year-old son, Childs, from the Scottish artist James Archer.

In his first four years of permanent residence in Pittsburgh, then, Frick's purchases were fairly conservative in taste and subject matter. They include four paintings by Pittsburgh artists (two still lifes, one family portrait, and one landscape), a second family portrait, and one oil and seven watercolors by traditional, European artists.

A three-year hiatus in major art purchases followed, perhaps attributable to Frick's increased business involvement in the mid-1880s. This changed in the summer of 1887, when he resigned from the presidency of The H. C. Frick Coke Company, and took his family on a European vacation. While in Germany, he purchased what was by far his most costly painting to date: J. G. Meyer von Bremen's *The Darlings*. Meyer von Bremen was a genre artist who studied in Düsseldorf and painted in the meticulously detailed style of that school. The title of the unidentified work, as well as the training of its artist, suggests that it was similar to the narrative paintings Frick purchased in 1881. On October 26, 1887, presumably on his return from Europe, Frick was in New York and purchased a painting by Tito Lessi, *A Man Reading*, from the gallery of Charles Sedelmeyer. Like Meyer von Bremen, Lessi was an academically trained artist whose genre scenes were carefully worked in a very meticulous, highly finished style. Both artists were popular among late-nineteenth-century collectors.

With these two substantial purchases, one might have thought that Frick's entry into the world of high-priced art collecting had begun and that other sought-after pieces would soon follow. But circumstances intervened, and the launching of a full-scale collection would have to wait another seven years. Back in Pittsburgh, Frick's business and personal interests took top priority; in January 1888, he resumed the presidency of the coke company and, by the next year, he was Chairman of the Board of Carnegie Brothers Steel. The years between 1887 and 1895 also saw the Homestead Steel Strike, the attempt on Frick's life, and the deaths of two of his children.

Records indicate that only four paintings were purchased during these years and their subjects were consistent with earlier purchases. In 1891, Frick bought a still life entitled *Peaches* by G.W.

Henry Clay Frick's circle of Pittsburgh friends included several artists, especially Joseph R. Woodwell, who appears in this photograph of an outdoor gathering. Left to right, *standing, William Frew, Woodwell, Henry Clay Frick; seated, Marika Ogiz (Helen's tutor), Margaret Woodwell, Emily Frew, Helen (on the ground), Adelaide Frick, and Virginia Frew (on the ground).*

Waters, an American-born, European-trained artist. Three years later, Frick made three purchases: March 22, 1894, a family portrait by Dr. Roseti, New York; *Still Life with Wine Bottle* by Antoine Vollon from Arnold and Tripp, Paris; and May 28, 1894, *Coming in from the Garden* by Ridgeway Knight from M. Knoedler & Company. Of these works only the Roseti was retained in the collection. The Knight painting, which was the earliest work of art Frick purchased from Knoedler's, was returned to the gallery—not a very auspicious beginning to what would become an extremely rewarding relationship between art gallery and patron.

In 1895, Frick began to give his collecting impulses, which had so far been sporadic, full rein.

That year alone, he purchased fifteen paintings and, until the turn of the century, continued to collect at a rate of one painting per month. Most acquisitions in 1895 were made through Knoedler's, and included contemporary European artists, primarily French, as well as painters from the Barbizon School. Among others, works by Rico, Bouguereau, Breton, Cazin, and Thaulow entered the collection. Frick did not forget his Pittsburgh dealer either; on April 24, 1895 he bought what would be the last major art purchase from Gillespie's: Jean-Baptiste Robie's *Flower Piece—Roses.*

As he actively set about to collect European art, Frick did not lose interest in certain Pittsburgh artists. In October of 1895 he purchased three paintings directly from the artists: *A Harvest Scene* by John W. Beatty, *Shepherd and Sheep* by A. Bryan Wall, and an unidentified landscape by Joseph R. Woodwell. At the same time, he may also have purchased the second Hetzel landscape, dated 1894, that remains in Clayton's collection.

Frick knew all four artists well. As stated earlier, his first dealings with Hetzel came immediately after he came to Pittsburgh and surely continued when he served on the Board of Trustees of The Pittsburgh School of Design for Women, where Hetzel taught. The three other artists were involved with Frick in overseeing what was to become Carnegie Institute. At least by October 1895, Frick was the Treasurer of the Board of Trustees of Carnegie Library. At the same time, Woodwell and Beatty were on the ''Art Committee'' of the ''Carnegie Art Galleries,'' where Beatty also served as director. In 1896, A. Bryan Wall succeeded his father on the Art Committee.

A September 16, 1895, letter to Roland Knoedler indicates that the friendships between Frick and these artists began even earlier. In the letter to his New York dealer, Frick speaks of some recent purchases and states, ''A number of my friends have already seen them, among others Woodwell, Beatty....'' Frick had numerous dealings with Beatty over the next few years as he generously lent his collection to exhibitions at the Carnegie Art Galleries. Beatty also occasionally advised Frick on art purchases. Their friendship continued after Frick left Pittsburgh for New York, and in 1908 Beatty sent a warmly inscribed etching of *Fishermen's Shacks, Traps, and Boats* to the Fricks as a Christmas present.

Woodwell also seems to have been particularly close to the Frick family. In Helen Clay Frick's memoirs, written in the 1950s, she speaks about her recollections of the artist:

Mr. and Mrs. Joseph R. Woodwell were also very good friends and lived only a few blocks away on Penn Avenue. Mr. Woodwell was an artist, and when my Father and I took walks together, we nearly always headed in the direction of his studio and spent hours there looking over his most recent pictures and listening to the tales he told of his early years as a student in Paris. Mr. Woodwell had known most of the painters of the Barbizon School and at this particular time, my

father's collection was predominantly of that school. Everytime a new painting was acquired at Clayton, Mr. Woodwell was the first to be invited to see it.

Three Woodwell paintings remain at Clayton. The earliest is entitled *Landscape with Carriage* and is dated 1895. This is probably not the one Frick purchased in 1895, but one he received in an exchange in 1897. In 1903 Frick purchased another landscape painting from the artist, probably *Landscape with Cypresses* now in the collection. A third painting, *Sand Dunes, Gloucester, Massachusetts*, was purchased from the artist in 1908.

The Woodwell, Hetzel, Beatty, and Wall paintings that remain in Clayton's collection are a permanent testament to Frick's early appreciation of the city's local talent. But by 1895, a full decade before the family took up residence in New York, Frick was acquiring almost all his art through New York dealers. It is quite significant that in 1896 Frick traded his two fruit paintings by A. Bryan Wall and George Hetzel for a fruit piece by the eighteenth-century Dutch artist, Jan van Os (cat. no. 45). This was Frick's first ''Old Master'' painting. Rembrandts, Titians, and Vermeers would follow, most of which were ushered into Frick's collection by Roland Knoedler and Charles Carstairs of M. Knoedler & Company. Thereafter, Gillespie's only packed and shipped Frick's paintings. But Pittsburgh is where Henry Clay Frick's love of art was kindled. And, as the letters and memoirs suggest, Pittsburgh's most outstanding artists contributed to Frick's appreciation of art while he was on his way to becoming one of America's greatest art collectors.

It is remarkable that every phase of Frick's collecting is represented at Clayton: early purchases for the apartment in the Monongahela House and for Clayton; later purchases originally intended for the family's New York residences; and purchases made for Eagle Rock, their summer home. Nowhere is Henry Clay Frick's evolving taste in collecting more evident, for here Western Pennsylvania landscapes, late-nineteenth-century salon pieces, Barbizon pastels, and significant Old Master portraits—all are at home at Clayton.

Kahren Jones Hellerstedt

Selection of Art from the Exhibition

29. *Landscape with River*

George Hetzel (1826, near Strasbourg, Alsace, France–1899, Somerset, Pennsylvania)

Oil on canvas
44½ in. x 29½ in. (113 cm. x 74.9 cm.)
Signed and dated lower right: *Geo. Hetzel 1880*
Provenance: S. Boyd and Company of Pittsburgh; purchased by Henry Clay Frick, February 12, 1881.

George Hetzel was one of the most popular and acclaimed artists to work in the Pittsburgh area in the latter half of the nineteenth century. Born near Strasbourg in Alsace, France, Hetzel came to Pittsburgh with his family at age two. He received his first artistic training as a house and sign painter and earned money by painting interior decorations for riverboats, cafes, and a local penitentiary. This income helped to finance two years of study at the Düsseldorf Academy, a school known for its precise, realistic style of landscape and genre painting. After his return to Pittsburgh in 1849, Hetzel painted portraits and still lifes which reflected this descriptive style. Although he continued to work with these motifs throughout his career, in the late 1850s Hetzel began to concentrate on landscapes of the southwestern Pennsylvania area. These represented his main interest and produced his greatest artistic success.

This landscape is one of a great number of works painted at Scalp Level, a mountain retreat in Cambria County. The ''Scalp Level School'' attracted many Pittsburgh artists who, unlike their contemporaries in the Hudson River School, chose to depict nature with a more intimate and meditative view. These artists were familiar with the work of the French Barbizon painters working in the forest of Fontainebleau, and their paintings reflected a Barbizon influence in a somber tonal quality, freer use of paint, and a somewhat solemn portrayal of nature.

At the Düsseldorf Academy, Hetzel learned to use dramatic effects of light and shade. He adapted this technique to his own personal style that focused on dimly lit woodland interiors. Hetzel often used the deep forest as an almost impenetrable backdrop through which patterns of light filter to the ground. This painting departs from this approach in both composition and quality of light. The viewer is offered an uninterrupted look through the trees which frame the scene, to follow the path of a stream as it reaches back toward a distant hillside. Both stream and sunlight originate somewhere beyond the trees, inviting the eye to travel through the space and to stop at rocks, trees, and rhododendron along the way.

The artist combines meticulous observation of natural light with the use of a variety of green, orange, and brown tones to create warmth in the areas bathed in light, and to produce the cool hues in the foreground shadows that envelope the viewer. It is this ability to surround, to draw the viewer into the landscape, that creates the perception that one has just emerged onto a scene, and that offers a look at nature that is both very direct and very private.

George Hetzel was the only painter of the Scalp Level School to gain national recognition in his day; in fact, the artist's first important sale was to Mrs. Abraham Lincoln. The purchase of *Landscape with River* in 1881 is Henry Clay Frick's earliest recorded purchase of a work of art.   N. G.

30. *Still Life*

William Michael Harnett (1848, Clonakilty, County Cork–1892, New York City)

Oil on panel
7½ in. x 9½ in. (19.1 cm. x 24.1 cm.)
Signed and dated lower left: *WM HARNETT* (in monogram) *1890*
Provenance: purchased from an unknown source by Henry Clay Frick, November 12, 1895.

Although he was born in Ireland and died in New York, William Michael Harnett spent his formative years in Philadelphia, where he must have seen *trompe l'oeil* paintings by Raphaelle Peale (1774-1825). Peale's still life paintings of the first quarter of the nineteenth century, with their consummate technique, precise style, and humble objects, were to find no equal until Harnett took up the genre six decades later.

Harnett produced only nine known paintings during the last four years of his short life. Suffering from rheumatism and renal failure, the artist painted but a single work in 1889; in 1890, he managed to complete three canvases, including the well-known *Faithful Colt,* and two small panels, of which this is one. *Still Life* is a close version, though only one-fourth the size, of a Harnett painting of 1890 entitled *Emblems of Peace* (Museum of Fine Arts, Springfield, Massachusetts). It is not, however, a copy. The leather- and vellum-bound books, Dutch jar, open blue tobacco box with shredded tobacco, and meerschaum pipe appear in both, but are slightly rearranged from one composition to the next. Other alterations occur as well: a piccolo replaces the flute in the Springfield work, and the book titles and tempo marks—all of which are quite readable on the large canvas—now have only an apparent legibility.

It is not unusual for Harnett to attach rather homey or nostalgic titles to his works of art, and it was the artist himself who entitled the Springfield canvas *Emblems of Peace.* The title suggests that literature, music, and art (represented by the painting itself) thrive in peacetime. The title, however, probably should not be used for the miniaturized version of the composition, for there are numerous paintings—filled with nearly identical objects—that Harnett did not feel compelled to christen with poetic titles.

As is typical of *tromp l'oeil* works, this painting depicts its objects in a shallow space. There is clearly a feeling of verisimilitude in this work, but its markedly reduced scale makes clear that here the artist is not attempting to deceive. One still marvels at the realistically, almost microscopically, rendered details: the split ivory head on the piccolo, the crackling of the jar's glazed finish, and the torn edges of the yellowed sheet-music. Harnett has assembled a group of well-used, apparently common things; yet, his choice of objects suggests taste, erudition, and refinement.

Tacked neatly in the corner on the reverse of the panel is the artist's calling card, which reads:

W. M. HARNETT
STUDIO 13   1227 BROADWAY
THIRD FLOOR   NEW YORK

The New York City directory lists Harnett's studio at this address from 1890 until his death in 1892. The card's presence suggests that the painting was purchased directly from the artist, although precisely from whom Mr. Frick bought it in 1895 is uncertain. The earliest photographs of Clayton show the painting hanging there; apparently, it has never left.   K. J. H.

31. *The Sower*

Jean-François Millet (1814, Gruchy–1875, Barbizon)

Pastel on tan wove paper
12⅛ in. x 9⅝ in. (30.8 cm. x 24.5 cm.)
Signed at lower right: *J. F. Millet*
Provenance: Alfred Sensier; Lebrun; M. Knoedler & Co., New York; purchased by Henry Clay Frick, March 8, 1899.

The theme of the solitary sower casting grain in a barren field preoccupied Jean-Francois Millet for over twenty years in paintings, drawings, and prints. This pastel is a later variant, c.1865, of Millet's great masterpiece (Museum of Fine Arts, Boston) painted fifteen years earlier and exhibited at the Salon of 1850-1851.

In the Boston painting, the peasant fills the canvas as he strides purposefully across a Norman field sowing winter wheat. Back lit by the last rays of the setting sun, his powerful figure dominates the composition while his face is hidden in the shadow cast by the brim of his hat. What distinguishes this figure from those represented in contemporary small-scale genre scenes is the dignity and resolve of the peasant who elevates an everyday chore to a rite. As Alexandra Murphy has stated, ''Sowing is the penultimate act of faith in man's battle to earn his daily bread, for potentially edible grain is flung to the winds, in the hope of harvests beyond the control of the sower.''

Although the pastel retains the painting's general compositional arrangement, there are changes that considerably alter its overall effect. Most significantly, the size of the sower in the pastel is reduced so that the figure no longer dominates the desolate landscape. And while the poses of both sowers are similar, the pastel figure's legs are placed closer together so that he now walks the clodded field less stridently than did his earlier counterpart in the painting.

The background farmer with the ox-drawn harrow appears on the horizon of both painting and pastel, but the setting has changed from Normandy to Barbizon. The specific site represented is the plain that joins Barbizon with Chailly, recognizable by the remains of the tower of Chailly. In the painting the landscape is bathed by the light of the setting sun; whether Millet intended the same effect for the pastel is difficult to ascertain because the paper has darkened and the color harmonies that originally existed in the sky have been disturbed.

A number of pastel versions of *The Sower* exist containing similar departures from Millet's famous painted version. Like the drawing discussed here, these later versions all de-emphasize the figure, making him more a part of the landscape in which he toils. Most of these drawings have a horizontal format which increases the expanse of tilled soil to both sides and further diminishes the figure's overall effect. When the original painting was exhibited at the Salon, its monumental sower was interpreted as everything from a quasi-religious figure to a protest on behalf of the contemporary proletariat. Throughout his life, Millet stressed that his work was not political. Perhaps his reduction of the size of his peasant suggests that his ultimate intention was to make no broader statement than to recognize the life-giving force of a peasant sowing seeds for next year's harvest.

This is one of three Millet drawings, including *Le Puy-de-Dôme* and *The Cow Herder*, purchased by Henry Clay Frick in 1899 for Clayton. K. J. H.

32. *La Fermière*

Jean-François Millet (1814, Gruchy–1875, Barbizon)

Pastel on blue grey wove paper
15½ in. x 20¾ in. (39.4 cm. x 52.7 cm.)
Signed at lower right: *J. F. Millet*
Provenance: Émile Gavet; Ernest May; Defoer Collection Sale, Galerie Georges Petit, Paris, May 22, 1886;
  M. Knoedler & Co., New York; purchased by Henry Clay Frick, October 7, 1897.

The theme of a young woman tending cows was a Millet favorite throughout his career. In 1859, Millet entered his controversial painting, *A Woman Pasturing Her Cow* (Musée de l'Ain, Bourg-en-Bresse) in the Salon; critical reaction was quite vociferous. As in the case of the earlier *Sower* (see discussion, cat. 31) viewers saw opposing social and political implications in the large-scale, heroically rendered peasant woman. Millet's later pastel versions of women cow herders, like his later renditions of sowers, feature smaller figures, more landscape, and little, if any, social commentary.

A frequently used compositional device of the artist is to isolate a solitary figure in a vast landscape. Here the small woman, who appears even smaller wedged between the hulking, bony frames of her two cows, stands before a seemingly endless plain watching a flock of birds in flight. The daunting, horizontal flatness of the pasture, however, is wonderfully relieved by the vertical stand of skeletal trees silhouetted against the bright sky.

In 1863, Millet produced a compositionally similar pastel (Museum of Fine Arts, Boston), that likewise includes a woman with one brown and one white cow, rendered by overlaying a detailed black crayon drawing with a few colors. Technically, it is less advanced than *La Fermière*, which must have been done several years later. In *La Fermière*, the pasture is built up with rapid flecks and strokes in a variety of colors. Besides the expected greens and browns, there are mauves, oranges, mustards, and pinks. The resulting grassland is visually exciting and makes a lively backdrop for the large, bulky shapes of the figure and animals. A particularly inspired detail that would appear to have no basis in visual reality is the long continuous band of pale lavender that runs the width of the drawing at the base of the trees. In these spontaneous, evocative touches of color, Millet seems to anticipate the next great school of French landscape painting, the Impressionists.

La Fermière is the first of nine Millet drawings known to have been purchased by Henry Clay Frick between 1897 and 1908.   K. J. H.

33. *Le Puy-de-Dôme*

Jean-François Millet (1814, Gruchy–1875, Barbizon)

Pastel on grey wove paper
18½ in. x 22⅛ in. (47 cm. x 56.2 cm.)
Signed at lower right: *J. F. Millet*
Provenance: Count Doria in 1887; M. Knoedler & Co., New York; purchased by Henry Clay Frick, August 21, 1899.

In June of 1866, and again in the summers of 1867 and 1868, Millet traveled to the mountains of central France with his wife in the hopes of improving her health at the spas in Vichy. Whenever he could get free, the artist explored the countryside in the surrounding Bourbonnais region and in the Auvergne as far as Clermont-Ferrand. Millet's nearly two hundred sketches of these locations attest to his fascination with the area, as well as to his growing interest in pure landscape. Many of the drawings are little more than a few rapid pencil strokes done in a small notebook; others are more complete and include notations about the region's vegetation and colors. Millet's on-site drawings served him well, for he used them with little alteration as models for almost fifty paintings and pastels.

The richly colored pastel, *Le Puy-de-Dôme,* is an example of a finished studio work based on Millet's travel sketches. The Puy-de-Dôme is the volcano without a crater that marks the highest point of the Puys mountain chain, about fifteen miles west of Clermont-Ferrand. The scene's rocky terrain is capped at the horizon by this impressive, grey massif enveloped in clouds. The dark brown area that also surrounds the mountain peak is not the result of an impending volcanic eruption, but rather an unfortunate darkening of the paper.

While her scrawny goats graze on the cliffs, a solitary goat herder sits and knits. Knitting is the constant companion of many of Millet's young shepherdesses, for there are few moments when the hands of these young peasant girls can afford to be idle. As in so many Millet compositions, the inclusion of a lone figure gives the work a meditative mood.

Despite the ruggedness of the jutting rocks, the vista is anything but bleak. This is due primarily to the bright, intense colors Millet has layered on the paper. Warm yellow and chartreuse vegetation surrounds the tiny female figure, who herself is dressed in clear blue and delicate pink. Rapid colorful pastel strokes enliven the taller foreground grasses, while the hills in the middle distance glow with a blue-green hue. Here Millet shows his mastery of the medium which he manipulates with apparent ease to suggest the variety of colors, textures, and atmospheric effects to be found on a warm spring day in the mountains.

Le Puy-de-Dôme is one of five Millet pastels known to have hung in the reception room at Clayton at the turn of the century.   K. J. H.

34. *The Knitting Lesson*

Jean-François Millet (1814, Gruchy–1875, Barbizon)

Black chalk on dark cream laid paper
14 in. x 11 in. (35.6 cm. x 27.9 cm.)
Signed at lower right: *J. F. Millet*
Provenance: Mr. Duz, 1887; Mrs. G. van den Eynde, 1897; E. J. van Wesselingh and Co., Amsterdam and London;
   M. Knoedler & Co., New York; purchased by Henry Clay Frick, October 14, 1898.

The theme of a mother teaching her daughter is one that Millet must have found particularly meaningful, for he returned to it many times during his career. Whether it was reading, sewing, or other handiwork, Millet depicted each task being carefully taught by a patient mother to her intent child. Although Millet's artistic inspiration for such quiet domestic scenes is generally acknowledged to be seventeenth-century Dutch genre painting and the work of Jean-Siméon Chardin, he need not have depended on earlier artistic representation: Millet's six daughters would have given him ample opportunity to witness these events first hand.

There are nine known versions of *The Knitting Lesson:* four paintings, three finished drawings, and two pages of compositional sketches. The present drawing, dated c.1858, is a final preparatory drawing for the painting in the Sterling and Francine Clark Art Institute (Williamstown, Massachusetts). The only differences that occur between the two are in the numerous household items that line the back wall of the modest interior. The mood in all of the versions, regardless of medium, is quiet and dignified as Millet stresses the virtue inherent in fulfilling simple domestic tasks.

The Knitting Lesson was among the earliest Millet drawings purchased by Henry Clay Frick for Clayton. It hung in the reception room of the house at least by 1900.   K. J. H.

35. *La Sortie*

Jean-François Millet (1814, Gruchy–1875, Barbizon)

Black and white chalk on cream color laid paper
15¼ in. x 12⁵⁄₁₆ in. (38.7 cm. x 31.3 cm.)
Signed lower right: *J. F. Millet*
Provenance: Émile Gavet until 1875; James Staats Forbes until 1904; Alice N. Lincoln, Manchester, Massachusetts; purchased by Henry Clay Frick, August 22, 1908.

Millet spent the last three decades of his life working from his cottage at Barbizon, surrounded by his wife and nine children—and later his grandchildren. Not unexpectedly, the constant activities of his family members found expression in his work. *La Sortie* (The Departure) depicts an event the artist must have witnessed countless times: a mother leaving for the market, taking with her the youngest child. The young mother's gesture is particularly touching as she walks the sunlit cottage path and takes a second to press the baby's cheek to her own. The woman's day began hours before, however, for the newly washed linens are spread over the bushes to dry.

La Sortie is thought to be one of a pair of drawings. Its mate, *Le Retour* (The Return), depicts the woman once more at home. The baby, exhausted by the day's activities, is rocked to sleep by its mother. Supper, probably bought earlier in the day, cooks in an iron kettle that is hanging in the fireplace.

La Sortie and *Le Retour* were among the more than ninety-five pastels created for Émile Gavet (1830-1904), who in September 1865 convinced Millet to work almost exclusively for him and almost exclusively in pastel. It is the last recorded Millet drawing purchased by Henry Clay Frick.

K. J. H.

36. *Bords de la Seine à Lavacourt*

Claude Monet (1840, Paris–1926, Giverny)

Oil on canvas
22⅞ in. x 31½ in. (58.1 cm. x 80 cm.)
Signed, lower left: *Claude Monet*
Provenance: Boussod, Valadon and Co.; Potter Palmer, Chicago, until 1894; Durand-Ruel and Sons;
  purchased by Henry Clay Frick, March 2, 1901.

This painting and its subject, a view of the town of Lavacourt from a bank of the Seine, stems from a time of dramatic change in both the artistic and emotional life of Claude Monet. By the late 1870s, when the work was painted, Monet had emerged as the leader, the strongest personality, and the most astute painter of the group of artists who would come to be called the Impressionists. Monet was one of the originators of the movement, and one of his canvases gave the group its name.

As a reaction to the sobriety of the Salon and its expectation that painting conform to idealized imagery and high narrative content, the Impressionists sought to show the world as it is actually perceived, not as a fixed image, but as many different glimpses of an ever-changing scene synthesized by a constantly moving eye. In the group's first independent exhibition in April 1874, Monet submitted *Impression, Sunrise,* which attracted such negative critical attention that the name became associated with the entire group of artists.

The pursuit of this spontaneity explains the desire of the Impressionists to paint outdoors. Monet was a very prolific *plein-air* painter, and it is almost certain, in view of its size, that this view of Lavacourt was painted outdoors. In the summer of 1879, he painted a great number of views of Lavacourt from the embankment in front of his house at Vétheuil. The foliage on the river in the foreground here differs from that in paintings of the same scene dated 1878 and 1880. This painting of the scene as dusk approaches on a hazy summer day is probably one of the many that was produced in 1879.

Monet moved to a tiny house in the small town of Vétheuil in the summer of 1878 with his wife Camille, eleven-year-old son Jean, infant son Michel, and the family of Ernest Hoschedé, a one-

time patron who had recently declared bankruptcy. The hardships involved in this uncomfortable living arrangement were compounded by Monet's own financial distress, Camille's failing health, and an amorous relationship between Monet and Alice Hoschedé. When the situation became unworkable, the Hoschedés left. Desperate to paint and to provide much needed income, Monet studied the shore across the river, remaining within reach of his family, which became increasingly dependent upon his care.

Following Camille's death in September of 1879, Monet painted little more than still-lifes. The Impressionist group had begun to disintegrate under the pressures of continued critical and public scorn. Prompted by his growing disaffection with the group, as well as by his financial desperation, Monet decided once again to submit work to the Salon. In a letter to his friend Théodore Duret in March 1880, Monet discussed his work on "three large canvasses, only two of which are for the Salon, because one of the three is too much to my taste to send. It would be refused, and I ought instead to do something more discreet, more bourgeois." The discreet, bourgeois painting he sent was *Lavacourt,* a large canvas painted in the studio, based on the studies made the previous year. Its acceptance into the Salon would initiate a more positive critical response, owing to its more traditional, descriptive approach in depicting the familiar scene.

Whatever compromises Monet may have made with *Lavacourt,* he achieved with this painting a degree of approval that made the critics and public more open to his work. This included a receptivity to work more to his taste, such as *Lavacourt's* companion piece *Sunset on the Seine, Winter.* But *Bords de la Seine à Lavacourt* also reflects a more

adventurous, changing style. Partly because of his frantic need to produce, he employed a more summary, suggestive way of rendering form, with attention focussed on the passing effects of light and atmospheric conditions. More varied than in the Salon piece *Lavacourt,* the color and brushstrokes work together to create a shimmering effect and to suggest a scene that is bathed in a warm, but fading light. The variation in the painting's surface, especially in the colors stroked over the visible underpainting of sky and water, is a precursor to the more sketchy style of the paintings from

Giverny in which the bare canvas becomes a part of the picture surface.

In 1895, Henry Clay Frick purchased an earlier Monet entitled *Argenteuil,* originally in the collection of a Mr. Nunez of Paris. It remained in his collection until 1909, when it was returned to the dealer L. Crist Delmonico in partial exchange for a painting by Aelbert Cuyp. It was later sold to a private collector in Switzerland. Mr. Frick purchased *Bords de la Seine à Lavacourt* in 1901 from Paul Durand-Ruel, the Parisian dealer who represented many of the Impressionists.   N. G.

37. *Christ and the Disciples at Emmaus*

Pascal-Adolphe-Jean Dagnan-Bouveret (1852, Paris–1929, Quincey)

Oil on panel
26½ in. x 37⅞ in. (67.3 cm. x 96.2 cm.)
Signed upper right: *PAJ Dagnan-B*
Provenance: Arthur Tooth and Sons, New York; purchased by Henry Clay Frick, December 9, 1898.

The paintings of Dagnan-Bouveret, one of the more conservative members of the French Academy, were highly prized during the late nineteenth century. A student of Gérôme and a friend of Bastien-Lepage, Dagnan-Bouveret won such honors as the second Grand Prix de Rome in 1876 and medals at the Salons of 1878 and 1880. However, changing taste has not been kind to this once-popular artist whom Henry Clay Frick knew personally.

Dagnan-Bouveret's original version of *Christ and the Disciples at Emmaus* was certainly the most unusual purchase made by Henry Clay Frick during his thirty-eight years of serious art collecting. The panel presently in Clayton's collection is a reduced replica by the artist of his huge (over 6½ feet x 9 feet) canvas painted in 1896-97 and presented in 1898 to Carnegie Institute, ''In Memory of Martha Howard Frick by Her Parents.'' Martha, Frick's oldest daughter, had died in 1891 at the age of six.

The original canvas, remarkable in Frick's 1898 collection for its large size, high purchase price, religious subject, and psychological impact, was indeed a departure from his earlier acquisitions, which tended to be moderately sized, modestly priced landscapes, portraits, still lifes, and genre scenes. In the summer of 1897, Frick apparently saw the incomplete painting in Dagnan-Bouveret's studio while visiting with Edmond Simon, the Paris agent for Arthur Tooth and Sons. Immediately struck by the work, Frick contracted to purchase the painting when it was finished.

Outstanding artistic examples of Christ at Emmaus by such well-known artists as Veronese, Caravaggio, and Rembrandt were certainly known to both the artist and the collector. The story as

recounted in the Gospel according to Saint Luke is as follows: after Christ's resurrection, he meets two pilgrims journeying to Emmaus who do not recognize him as the risen Christ until he breaks bread at supper, after which he instantly ''vanished out of their sight'' (Luke 24:31). This image of miraculous apparition and disappearance apparently touched a responsive chord in the collector, for in 1892, when Frick lay close to death from an attempted assassination, he was ''dazzled'' by the image of his deceased daughter.

Both original and replica are dominated by the powerful figure of Christ, resplendent in his white robe and fiery orange hair. His pose clearly derives from the Christ-figure in Leonardo's *Last Supper*. The blinding radiance that envelops Christ's head suggests his dematerialization as he vanishes. Although the two astonished pilgrims in Dagnan-Bouveret's work react to the miracle before them, they are certainly more subdued than are their stunned counterparts in Caravaggio's and Rembrandt's versions.

The depiction of Dagnan-Bouveret's servant girl also differs from earlier prototypes. Despite the fact that serving people are not mentioned in the Biblical account of the supper at Emmaus, they do appear in most earlier pictorial renditions. In these —unlike the girl in Dagnan-Bouveret's canvas— the servants are usually unaware of the miracle and go quietly about their work. Dagnan-Bouveret's decision to include the servant girl among those who recognize Christ's divinity may be what moved a Pittsburgh critic in 1898 to associate this girl with Martha.

It is the three remaining figures to the right of the composition that proved to be the source of controversy when the painting was unveiled.

The man, wife, and child in contemporary dress depict none other than the artist and his family. Although a critic for the *Chicago Tribune* would call their appearance a ''Shock'' as well as ''Scandalous and Sacrilegious,'' the inclusion of contemporary figures at religious scenes has a long, rich tradition in Western art. Veronese depicted himself and his family at the Emmaus supper (Louvre), and such artists as Botticelli, Michelangelo, and especially Rembrandt made frequent cameo appearances in their religious compositions. Often these self-inclusions represented little more than the artist's signature, however, there were occasions when artists had very specific, profound reasons for depicting themselves in sacred scenes. Dagnan-Bouveret was quite clear about his own appearance here:

Throughout the whole course of the present century, philosophy and science have, one after the other, entered into a struggle against religion. Have the scholars and philosophers succeeded in giving satisfaction to the human soul? I don't believe it. The figure of Christ remains, then, after 1900 years, as effulgent as ever; his rule of morals as sublime as ever. To receive his word, woman still kneels down without discussion, and her child, without understanding it, kneels also by her side. But man, after all these troubles, after all these doubts and all these denials, can no longer kneel as he once did. His brow is careworn, anxiety has desolated his heart.

Thus, this work has the distinction of being a personal statement for both the man who painted it, and the man who purchased it. The replica has remained at Clayton since 1898.   K. J. H.

38. *Portrait of the Hon. John Hamilton*

William Hogarth (1697, London–1764, London)

Oil on canvas
28¾ in. x 24¼ in. (72.1 cm. x 61.6 cm.)
Unsigned
Provenance: John James Hamilton (son of sitter, ninth Earl and first Marquess of Abercorn);
    James Hamilton (grandson of sitter, second Marquess and first Duke of Abercorn); George Douglas Hamilton;
    Edward R. Bacon until 1915; Mrs. Walter Rathbone Bacon; purchased by Henry Clay Frick, 1918.

The Hamilton family, whose succeeding generations have carried the titles of Earl, Marquess, and Duke of Abercorn, retained this portrait in their collection until the beginning of the twentieth century. It was exhibited at the Royal Academy in London as early as 1875. The painting's uninterrupted provenance makes secure the identification of the sitter as the Hon. John Hamilton, the second son of the seventh Earl of Abercorn. Hamilton, a captain in the Royal Navy, married Harriet Eliot, the widow of Richard Eliot, Esq. (M.P. for Port Eliot, Cornwall) in 1749. He drowned off the coast of Portsmouth on December 18, 1755.

The artist, William Hogarth, is best known for his biting, satirical paintings and prints lampooning the fashion and mores of eighteenth-century English society. Less well known, but just as notable, are Hogarth's portraits, for the same keen sense of observation that made him an excellent satirist enabled him to capture a good likeness.

Stylistically, Hogarth's *Portrait of the Hon. John Hamilton* can be dated to c.1740. Most of Hogarth's single portraits are dated between 1738 and 1743, when the artist found that small portraits were more readily commissioned, more financially rewarding, and faster and easier to execute than his earlier multi-figured conversation pieces and comic contemporary histories. During these years, Hogarth's single portraits were primarily of clergymen, professionals, and merchants. Only rarely did a nobleman sit for him.

Hogarth's portrayal of his sitters was straightforward and uninflated. He consciously strove to set aside the established, somewhat mechanical, formulas for portraiture, which dictated the use of a standardized oval face, long nose, and narrow eyes. Hogarth's painted faces, on the contrary, are round and beaming. They suggest good health, vitality, and cheerfulness.

These characteristics are certainly evident in the painting of John Hamilton whose full, fleshy mouth, rosy cheeks, and clear blue eyes highlight his handsome face. As in so many of Hogarth's portraits from this period, there are no allusions to Hamilton's rank. Even the background is monochromatic, enlivened only by an unadorned column. But the work is far from dull. The sitter's informal pose, accented by his unbuttoned coat, as well as his forthright expression create a lively individual presence.

Further enhancing this sense of immediacy is Hogarth's handling of paint. The brushstrokes are broad and quickly worked. Particularly notable is the bravura brushwork of the dazzling waistcoat: the multi-colored embroidered flowers shimmer against the garment's gold scalloped edging. The same virtuosity extends to the flowing white jabot and cuffs that enliven the blue coat. It is a testament to the artist's talent as a portraitist that the colorful liveliness of the fabrics does not eclipse the painted face of John Hamilton, which remains the focus of the painting.

This was one of several outstanding portraits by prominent English artists—including Romney, Reynolds, and Gainsborough—acquired in 1918 by Henry Clay Frick.

K. J. H.

39. *Sir Joshua Vanneck and His Family of Roehampton House, Putney*

Arthur Devis (1708, Preston–1787, London)

Oil on canvas
57½ in. x 55¾ in. (146.1 cm. x 141.6 cm.)
Signed and dated on tree trunk: *Ar Devis fe. 1752*
Provenance: By descent to Reginald Henry Nevill (grandson of Richard Walpole); Lady Dorothy Nevill (1826-1916); Christie's, June 13, 1913, lot 74; M. Knoedler & Co., New York; purchased by Henry Clay Frick, January 1916.

This painting is an outstanding example of the *conversation piece*, a genre of painting that originated in the Netherlands, flourished in eighteenth-century England, and declined only with the invention of photography. The genre can best be described as an informal family portrait that includes at least two family members who by their gaze or gesture could be engaged in conversation.

The extended family represented here is that of Sir Joshua Vanneck (d. 1777), whose name reflects his Dutch ancestry. Sir Joshua, a prosperous international financier, was made a Baronet in 1751; this honor could have occasioned the commissioning of the painting the following year. Although no contemporary account exists to identify each sitter, the assembled group probably represents Sir Joshua, who stands to the left, Mrs. De La Mont (his sister?), four Vanneck daughters, two sons, and two sons-in-law. The married couples would be Elizabeth and her husband the Hon. Thomas Walpole (1727-1803, Whig M.P., 1754-1784), and Anna Maria Cornelia and her husband Henry Uhthoff. The remaining children would be Gertrude, Joshua (d.1816), Gerard (1743?-1791, M.P. for Dunwich, 1768-1790), and Margaret, Sir Joshua's youngest daughter, who is seated on the ground. Five or six years after the portrait was painted, Margaret married Richard Walpole (1728-1798).

As befits a true conversation piece, the setting is a recognizable location associated with the sitters; most often it alludes to the family's prosperity. Here the Vannecks pose on the grounds of their estate, Roehampton House, in Putney near London. The site is identified by the accurately rendered bridge and town church. In 1778 the estate was described by Horace Walpole, the great chronicler of eighteenth-century England's history,

politics, and social life, as a ''beautiful terrace on the Thames with forty acres of ground.''

Horace Walpole's name has surfaced more than once in connection with this painting, for family tradition, followed by a number of early authors, has identified the seated man on the right as Horace, rather than his first cousin Thomas Walpole. No evidence exists, however, to support this identification. Horace Walpole was not known to be an intimate friend of the Vannecks, and it is inconceivable that he would have been included in a private family portrait—let alone in such a prominent position.

The painting is remarkable not only for the accomplishments of its sitters or would-be sitters, for it is one of Arthur Devis's most complex conversation pieces. Each figure exemplifies the artist's exaggerated stylization of the human form, which was at no time more pronounced than in the early 1750s. Young and old, male and female, are all depicted with small oval heads, tubular arms and legs, and dainty hands and feet. The women's figures are emphatically geometricized with their v-shaped wasp waists, square necklines, and box-like panniers.

The manipulation of the figures is extended to their poses, for despite the air of informality suggested by the outdoor setting, doffed hats, sun-bonnets, and forgotten gloves, there is no sense of relaxation among the family members. Each is separate and distinct, frozen into a carefully arranged tableau. The ten figures, in fact, form a narrow oval that stretches the width of the canvas, anchored at the left by the vertical figure of Sir Joshua and at the right by his seated son-in-law. The oval table at the center of the group reinforces the compositional arrangement. Nor is any gesture haphazard: each turn of the head and placement

of hands is controlled to suggest refinement.

The landscape is subjected to similar manipulation. The almost square canvas is bisected by a horizon of trees and hills. Diagonals into the distance, formed by the row of trees on the left, the edge of the bowling green, and the river wall are aligned so that they all lead to the tall church tower. Even the summer tent at the end of the green is carefully located so that it frames the head of the centrally placed daughter.

Despite the artist's controlling hand, the paint-ing maintains its freshness. This is due largely to Devis's choice of bright clear colors, especially in the brilliantly painted fabrics. The shimmering gold and silver satins, frothy transparent netting, and sparkling patterns lend an air of gaiety to the proceedings. The liveliness and virtuosity within a controlled composition are responsible for this painting's reputation as one of the artist's finest.

This is the only *conversation piece* among Henry Clay Frick's extensive collection of English portraits in Pittsburgh and New York. K. J. H.

40. *Portrait of Sir George Howland Beaumont*

Sir Joshua Reynolds (1723, Plympton–1792, London)

Oil on canvas
29⅜ in. x 24½ in. (74.6 cm. x 62.2 cm.)
Unsigned
Provenance: Sir George Beaumont; Beaumont family; M. Knoedler & Co., New York;
   purchased by Henry Clay Frick, December 9, 1902.

A contemporary description of Sir George Howland Beaumont (1753-1827) described the man, without reservation, as "the leader of taste in the fashionable world." Even a cursory look at Beaumont's interests and achievements suggests that this is not an unreasonable assessment. A landscape artist, friend and patron of artists and writers, connoisseur and collector of Old Master paintings, and Member of Parliament, Beaumont assured himself of a place in history by bequeathing to his country the sixteen paintings that constituted the foundation of the National Gallery in London. Constable, Gainsborough, Wordsworth, and Coleridge were among his circle of notable friends. Reminiscing about Beaumont to Wordsworth in 1836, Constable wrote: "I feel that I am indebted to him for what I am as an artist"— quite a tribute from a man who was never able to sell Beaumont a painting.

Of all the outstanding men of arts and letters with whom Beaumont associated, it was Sir Joshua Reynolds who influenced him most deeply. Beaumont was introduced to Reynolds while still a student, and over the years Reynolds became his confidant and advisor. That Beaumont became passionately committed to the creation and collection of art is, in large part, due to the guidance he received from Reynolds.

Reynolds undoubtedly discussed technical aspects of painting with Beaumont and counseled him on his own work. Reynolds, whose technique has always been considered idiosyncratic, advised Beaumont: "Mix a little wax with your colors, but don't tell anybody." When Beaumont later suggested that the concoctions prescribed by the master would crack, Reynolds responded simply,

"All good pictures crack." Regardless of Beaumont's reservations, he consistently backed his mentor, and on many occasions rose to defend Reynolds's eccentric studio practices. When one couple chose George Romney to paint their daughter for fear that a Reynolds portrait would fade, Beaumont quickly countered, "No matter, take the chance; even a faded picture from Reynolds will be the finest thing you can have."

As close as these two men were, it is remarkable that this is the only known portrait of Beaumont by Reynolds. Beaumont sat for the portrait in 1787, and in July of the same year paid the artist's bill of £52 10s. The year after its completion, Reynolds exhibited the portrait at the Royal Academy; thereafter, Beaumont's heirs regularly loaned it to important exhibitions. Reynolds's image of Beaumont also was circulated through three engravings.

Reynolds's portrait of his thirty-four-year-old friend exhibits the clarity of tone, easy directness, and exciting paint surface typical of the portraits from the last decade of his life. The restricted colors of the figure and costume are enlivened by the rich, red backdrop. These color harmonies are repeated in a later portrait of Beaumont by John Hoppner (The National Gallery, London), who likewise included a sketchy red background behind the black and white dressed figure.

In the first years of this century, Henry Clay Frick purchased portraits by many well-known, eighteenth-century English artists, including Reynolds, Romney, and Gainsborough. In 1915, this portrait hung with a Reynolds portrait of Lady Beaumont (cat. no. 41) in the library at 1 East 70th Street, New York.   K. J. H.

41. *Portrait of Lady Beaumont*

Sir Joshua Reynolds (1723, Plympton–1792, London)

Oil on canvas
29⅜ in. x 24½ in. (74.6 cm. x 62.2 cm.)
Unsigned
Provenance: Sir George Beaumont; Beaumont family; M. Knoedler & Co., New York;
   purchased by Henry Clay Frick, December 9, 1902.

On May 6, 1778, Sir George Beaumont (cat. no. 40) married Margaret Willes (1758-1829), granddaughter of the controversial Lord Chief Justice John Willes, who was satirized in Hogarth's *The Bench*. The wedding marked the beginning of the couple's lifelong devotion to each other and the arts. Attractive and enthusiastic, Lady Beaumont was described by a contemporary, Mary Hartley, as a "young woman with some genius and a prodigious eagerness for knowledge and information." The perfect mate to her cosmopolitan husband, she took on his interests as her own. So intent was Margaret to complement Lord Beaumont, that Miss Hartley felt it necessary to add: "her greatest object seems to be the preservation of her husband's affection."

Lady Beaumont was interested in all of the arts. Together with her husband, she learned to draw, performed in theatricals, and developed such a taste in music that Coleridge remarked to Wordsworth, "One may wind her up with any music, but music it must be, of one sort or other." Lady Beaumont also became as skilled an art connoisseur as her husband, for it was she who bought the most significant of the sixteen paintings bequeathed by Beaumont to the nation: Rubens's *Château at Steen*.

Because of Sir George Beaumont's longstanding friendship with Reynolds, it is not surprising that his wife sat for a portrait by the master shortly after their marriage. Reynolds recorded sittings by Lady Beaumont in 1778; March 1779; and March 1780. He was paid £40 in 1778 and £30 in 1779. When the painting was exhibited at the Royal Academy in 1780, the reviewer in the *Morning Chronicle* gushed: "The portrait of Lady Beaumont, which has a wonderful effect, excites fresh astonishment at the magic power of the pencil of this artist."

This portrait has an interesting history. Because of the multiple sittings and payments, most historians have assumed the existence of two, nearly identical, Reynolds portraits of Lady Beaumont, one of which is lost. This hypothesis appeared to be confirmed by a mezzotint copy showing Lady Beaumont in the same pose but with a different hairstyle. It took two centuries and an overzealous restorer to clear up the matter.

The composition, as completed in 1780, was copied in a mezzotint by J. R. Smith; it matches the present portrait. At some later date, however, the portrait was altered, certainly by Reynolds himself, and most likely in 1787, when Reynolds painted Sir George Beaumont. In order to make the two Beaumont portraits look more like a pair, the oval framework in Lady Beaumont's painting was minimized because her husband's portrait was not done in an oval format. More noticeably, Lady Beaumont's hairstyle was brought up to date by lowering her bouffant hairdo and replacing her white headpiece with a plain, dark bonnet.

This is how Lady Beaumont's portrait appeared when Mr. Frick purchased it in 1902. As late as 1941, when the painting was published by Ellis Waterhouse in his monograph on Reynolds, Lady Beaumont still sported her small bonnet and late-1780s hairstyle. Sometime thereafter, the painting was cleaned and Reynolds's later alterations, probably believed to be by a later restorer, were removed to reveal a portrait hidden since the eighteenth century.

K. J. H.

42. *Portrait of Richard Brinsley Sheridan*

Thomas Gainsborough (1727, Sudbury–1788, London)

Oil on canvas
28 in. x 24 in. (71.1 cm. x 61 cm.)
Unsigned
Provenance: Sir Robert Peel, Bart., until 1897; Edward R. Bacon, until 1915; Mrs. Walter Rathbone Bacon;
   purchased by Henry Clay Frick, 1918.

Richard Brinsley Sheridan (1751-1816) was an eminent parliamentary orator as well as the author of such comedies as *The Rivals* and *The School for Scandal.* He was also a member of the remarkable circle of writers and artists, including Wordsworth, Coleridge, Reynolds, Constable, and Gainsborough, who frequented the Grosvenor Square house of Sir George Beaumont (cat. no. 40). Gainsborough's close relationship with Sheridan began years before, however, when they met at the home of Thomas Linley, a composer and music teacher in Bath. Linley had a beautiful, talented daughter, Elizabeth Ann (1754-1792), who was described by a contemporary bishop as, ''the connecting link between woman and angel.'' Her exquisite singing voice, which enchanted the music-loving Gainsborough, led her to critical acclaim on the London stage while she was still in her teens. Needless to say, Elizabeth had many suitors, all of whom she rebuffed until she eloped with the dashing Sheridan in 1772. After their marriage, Mrs. Sheridan put aside her career to look after the accounts of the Drury Lane Theater, which her husband managed.

The names of Sheridan and Gainsborough are forever linked through a somewhat bizarre anecdote told by Beaumont to Allan Cunningham, an early biographer of the artist. Gainsborough, while dining with Beaumont and Sheridan, had a premonition of his death. Taking Sheridan out of the room, the artist confided:

Now don't laugh but listen. I shall die soon—I know it —I feel it—I have less time to live than my looks infer —but for this I care not. What oppresses my mind is this: I have many acquaintances and few friends; and as I wish to have one worthy man to accompany me to the grave, I am desirous of bespeaking you—Will you come—Aye or no?

Sheridan, of course, agreed, and Gainsborough's melancholia immediately disappeared. Ironically, it was while attending one of Sheridan's spirited orations at the sensational impeachment trial of Warren Hastings at Westminster Hall that Gainsborough first felt the cancer symptoms that would shortly claim his life.

At about the same time that Gainsborough finished his spectacular full-length portrait of Elizabeth Sheridan, c.1786 (National Gallery, Washington), he undertook this portrait of her husband. It is a good example of the bust-length portraits in feigned ovals which the artist produced in great numbers. Modest in size, they are more informal and intimate than Gainsborough's large-scale works.

Gainsborough's well-known ability to capture his sitter's likeness, assures us that Sheridan was a handsome man with sensitive features and a somewhat wistful expression. Although his face is rendered with small, careful strokes, Sheridan's hair and clothes display Gainsborough's favorite sketchy technique, which features the vigorous brushwork thought to be quite unorthodox by fellow members of the Royal Academy.

The Portrait of Richard Brinsley Sheridan is the last of seven Gainsborough works purchased by Henry Clay Frick between 1903 and 1918.   K. J. H.

43. *Portrait of the Marquise du Blaizel*

Sir Thomas Lawrence (1769, Bristol–1830, London)

Oil on canvas
29¼ in. x 24¼ in. (74.3 cm. x 61.6 cm.)
Unsigned
Provenance: Private collection, France; M. Knoedler & Co., New York; purchased by
  Henry Clay Frick, March 15, 1902.

The elegant woman in this portrait is believed to be a member of the Blaizel family, one of the oldest and most distinguished in Picardy, France. Originating with the dukes of Brabant, the house of Blaizel was established before the reign of Louis IX (1226-1270). In 1714, the hereditary title of Marquis of the Holy Roman Empire was also bestowed on the Blaizels.

The artist, Sir Thomas Lawrence, was an exceptional portraitist who was appointed Painter in Ordinary to the King when only twenty-two, and elected to the Royal Academy at twenty-four. On the Continent, Lawrence achieved a popularity unmatched by any earlier English painter.

Lawrence painted the Marquise du Blaisel in 1825 in Paris, where he had gone on commission from George IV to paint the French king, Charles X. While there, he painted several portraits of members of the French aristocracy, including the *Portrait of Marie Caroline, Duchesse de Berri.* That painting is typical of his work from the 1820s, which features modish portraits of society women elegantly posed and dressed. Their flowing lines, fluid paint, and refined color are part of Lawrence's final development as an artist.

The *Portrait of the Marquise du Blaizel* exhibits these same characteristics. In this portrait, Lawrence posed the woman in profile to empha-size the comely shape and elongated neck she may or may not have possessed. Her head tilts provocatively toward the viewer. Her white gown, tightly belted with a satin cummerbund, is overlaid with transparent chiffon and set off by a deep blue garment. Despite the liveliness of the rest of the portrait, it is, of course, the woman's picture hat that steals the show. Its wide satin and chiffon ribbons, caught at the top in billowing bows, stream down to frame her face. The loops, twists, and turns of this frothy, millinery confection give the portrait a lively silhouette.

The landscape background, which enhances the lyricism of the painting, sweeps back uninterrupted to a distant, evocative horizon. No grand manner devices alter the mood, for in place of the draped column that provided a backdrop for centuries of aristocratic portraits, Lawrence has painted only a slender tree trunk.

This painting is one of two similar female portraits by Lawrence acquired within two years of one another by Mr. Frick. *The Portrait of Julia, Lady Peel* (The Frick Collection, New York), purchased in 1904, was painted in 1827, two years after the completion of the *Portrait of the Marquise du Blaizel.* Lady Peel also wears an extravagant hat, this time adorned with cascading scarlet feathers and a jeweled buckle.   K. J. H.

44. *View of the Grand Canal at San Geremia*

Francesco Guardi (1712, Venice–1793, Venice)

Oil on canvas
24¾ in. x 30¾ in. (62.9 cm. x 78.1 cm.)
Signed above doorway at left: *Franc. Guardi*
Provenance: Edward R. Bacon, until 1915; Mrs. Walter Rathbone Bacon; purchased by Henry Clay Frick, 1918.

Francesco Guardi, who was born and died in Venice, left a dazzling pictorial record of the eighteenth-century city. Guardi only began painting *vedute*, or views, rather late in his artistic career, about 1760, after working primarily as a history painter in the Guardi family studio. His abrupt change in direction can perhaps be explained by the enormous success enjoyed by Antonio Canaletto's (1697-1768) painted city views. Guardi's initial attempts at Venetian vistas were largely dependent on his study of Canaletto's *oeuvre*, and often he borrowed specific motifs from the elder artist's compositions. The two artists' paintings, however, are easy to distinguish. Canaletto constructed his compositions in an exacting manner, frequently using optical devices to ensure accuracy. Although Guardi initially followed this structured approach, he quickly abandoned it in favor of a more lyrical style that featured spontaneous, bravura brushwork and glittering lighting effects.

Guardi's mature style is apparent in this painting, which captures the spectacle of Venetian life. The area around the Cannaregio, the canal that opens up in the painting's center, is not a popular tourist site; Guardi's choice of the view may have been inspired by Canaletto's painting of the same scene completed thirty years earlier (Buckingham Palace, London).

It is certain that Guardi visited the actual site, for he made a lively preliminary drawing of it (Museo Correr, Venice). Guardi's view also includes the reconstruction in progress on the Church of San Geremia, not apparent in Canaletto's earlier painting. While San Geremia's prominent thirteenth-century Romanesque campanile was retained, the rest of the church was demolished in 1753; the new choir can be seen under construction at the left. Another notable landmark is Giovanni Marchiori's statue of St. John Nepomuk, which stands at the entrance to the Cannaregio. Marking the opposite side of the canal's entrance is the Palazzo Querini detti Papozze, while behind the statue of the saint is the Palazzo Labia, built in 1720.

A larger version of this view by Guardi hangs in the Alte Pinakothek in Munich. The major difference between the two works is that Guardi increased the width of the Grand Canal in the foreground of the present painting, thereby easing the congestion of the frenetic canal traffic and calming the scene.

This is one of three Guardi canal scenes purchased by Henry Clay Frick.   K. J. H.

45. *Still Life with Fruit*

Jan van Os (1744, Middleharnis–1808, The Hague)

Oil on canvas
27⅜ in. x 22¾ in. (69.5 cm. x 57.8 cm.)
Signed and dated center: *J Van Os fecit 1769*
Provenance: Quarles van Ufford, The Hague, Holland; Gross & Van Gigch, Pittsburgh;
  purchased by Henry Clay Frick, February 5, 1896.

The outstanding tradition of Netherlandish flower painting, which first bloomed with Jan Brueghel the Elder (1570-1645) and Ambrosius Bosschaert (1573-1621) and fully blossomed with Jan van Huysum (1682-1749), had its final flourish with Jan van Os. In this artist's fruit and flower pieces, his technical skill and creativity combine to produce dazzling paintings that have been sought after by collectors ever since they were created.

Van Os's style, which derives from that of his elder countryman Jan van Huysum, includes the painstaking detail so beloved by the Dutch. In this painting even the smallest objects, like the insects that light on the fruit, snails that creep along the branches, and water droplets that condense on the ledge, are perfectly delineated. Along with this exacting style, van Os also reused a number of van Huysum's standard motifs: the marble ledge, vase with *bas* relief, landscape background with statues, and many identical floral specimens.

Although the specific items that make up van Os's painting are realistically rendered, the composition they inhabit is not. As is typical of Dutch flower painters, van Os never painted from a model. This is clear from the assortment of spring flowers and late summer fruit that make up each painting. Rather, he made detailed watercolor studies of each specimen in its season and later combined them into fantastic arrangements.

And no florist, however skilled, could have arranged such a bouquet. Blossoms appear suspended in mid-air, succulent green grapes hover unsupported, and ripe cantaloupe and pomegranates turn improbably toward the viewer to reveal their seeded interiors. But his dramatic display is in no danger of collapse, for anchoring this dynamic pyramid of luscious fruits and flowers is a heavy marble ledge that stretches the width of the canvas.

Equally unnaturalistic are the still life's loud and brilliant colors. The pineapple glows before a flat blue sky; the small sprig of gooseberries shines like a string of opalescent pearls. Lighting is also capricious. Objects that appear to be spot-lighted throw no appreciable shadows, while other fruits and flowers languish in inexplicable darkness.

In many early seventeenth-century Dutch flower pieces, objects such as snails, butterflies, and pomegranates would have had moralistic or emblematic associations. In van Os's painting, however, any symbolic meaning these items may have carried is long since lost. Van Os's paintings are first and foremost superbly decorative. They are perhaps best appreciated as decorative accents in private homes, which explains the artist's long-standing popularity among private collectors.

This was one of three still life paintings that hung in the breakfast room at Clayton.   K. J. H.

SELECTED BIBLIOGRAPHY

The Helen Clay Frick Foundation Archives provided primary documentation for all essays and catalogue entries.

The Family

American Biographies (Washington, D.C., 1952).

John A. Brashear, The Autobiography of a Man Who Loved the Stars (New York, 1924).

James Howard Bridge, Inside History of the Carnegie Steel Company (New York, 1903).

Encyclopedia of Pennsylvania Biography (New York, 1967).

George Harvey, Henry Clay Frick, The Man (New York and London, 1928).

Ellen M. Rosenthal, ''Everyday Life at Clayton'' (Unpublished Lecture, 1987).

Joseph Frazier Wall, Andrew Carnegie (New York, 1970).

The House

Paul Atterbury and Elizabeth Aslin, Minton, 1798-1910 (Victoria and Albert Museum, London, 1976).

Claude Blair, ed., The History of Silver (New York, 1987).

D. B. Burke, et al, In Pursuit of Beauty: Americans and the Aesthetic Movement, ex. cat. The Metropolitan Museum of Art (New York, 1987).

Charles H. Carpenter, Jr., with Mary Grace Carpenter, Tiffany Silver (New York, 1978).

Charles H. Carpenter, Gorham Silver 1831-1981 (New York, 1982).

Charles H. Carpenter, Jr., and Janet Zapata, The Silver of Tiffany & Co., ex. cat. Museum of Fine Arts (Boston, Massachusetts, 1987).

Clifford Edward Clark, Jr., The American Family Home, 1800-1960 (Chapel Hill and London, 1986).

Collection Connaissance des Arts, [P. Fregnac and J. Meuvert authors], French Cabinet Makers of the Eighteenth Century (New York, 1965).

Geoffrey de Bellaique, The James A. de Rothschild Collection at Waddesdon Manor: French Furniture and Gilt Bronzes, (Fribourg, Switzerland, 1974).

Ellen Paul Denker, After the Chinese Taste: China's Influence in America, 1730-1930, ex. cat. Peabody Museum of Salem (Salem, Massachusetts, 1985).

Lu Donnelly, Clayton Building Documentation (Unpublished, September, 1985).

Eastlake-Influenced American Furniture 1870-1890, ex. cat. The Hudson River Museum (Yonkers, New York, 1973).

Svend Eriksen, Sèvres Porcelain (Paris, 1968).

Desmond Eyles, Royal Doulton 1815-1965: The Rise and Expansion of the Royal Doulton Potteries (London, 1965).

Antoinette Fay-Hallé and Barbara Mundt, Porcelain of the Nineteenth Century (New York, 1983).

F. Brayshaw Gilhespy, and Dorothy Budd, Royal Crown Derby China from 1876 to the Present Day (London, 1964).

Sidney M. Goldstein, Leonard S. Rakow, and Juliette K. Rakow, Cameo Glass: Masterpieces from 2000 Years of Glassmaking (Corning Museum of Glass, Corning, New York, 1982).

Carl Hernmarch, The Art of the European Silversmith (New York, 1977).

Llewellynn Jewitt, The Ceramic Art of Great Britain, 2nd edition, revised (New York, 1883).

Clay Lancaster, The Japanese Influence in America (New York, 1983).

Edgar de Noailles Mayhew and Minor Myers, Jr., A Documentary History of American Interiors: From the Colonial Era to 1915 (New York, 1980).

Herbert Peck, The Book of Rockwood Pottery (New York, 1968).

Dorothy T. Rainwater, Encyclopedia of American Silver Manufacturers (Hanover, Pennsylvania, 1966).

Henry Sandon, Royal Worcester Porcelain from 1862 to the Present Day, 3rd edition (London, 1978).

Harriet Prescott Spofford, Art Decoration Applied to Furniture (New York, 1878).

The Quest for Unity: American Art between World's Fairs 1876-1893, ex. cat. The Detroit Institute of Arts (Detroit, Michigan, 1983).

Pierre Verlet, Les Bronzes Dorés Française du XVIIIᵉ Siecle (Paris, 1987).

Phelps Warren, Irish Glass: The Age of Exuberance (London, 1970).

Edith Wharton, and Ogden Codman, The Decoration of Houses (New York, 1897).

The Clothing Collection

Alison Gernsheim, Victorian and Edwardian Fashion a Photographic Survey (New York, 1963).

Judith Jerde, ''Assessment of the Frick Clothing Collection, a Photographic Survey'' (Unpublished Paper, 1985).

The Young Collector

Gillian Hirth Bennet, essay from Art in Nineteenth-Century Pittsburgh (Pittsburgh, Pennsylvania, 1977).

Paul A. Chew, ed., Southwestern Pennsylvania Painters 1800-1945 (The Westmoreland County Museum of Art, Greensburg, Pennsylvania, 1981).

Nancy Colvin, ''Scalp Level Artists,'' Carnegie Magazine, LVII (Sept./Oct. 1984), pp. 14-20.

Alfred Frankenstein, After the Hunt: William Harnett and other American Still Life Painters 1870-1900 (Berkeley and Los Angeles, 1969).

Kenneth Garlick, Sir Thomas Lawrence (London, 1954).

John House, Monet: Nature into Art (New Haven and London, 1986).

Joel Isaacson, Observation and Reflection: Claude Monet (London, 1978).

Peter Mitchell, Jan van Os 1744-1808 (Leigh-on-Sea, 1968).

Antonio Morassi, Guardi: Antonio e Francesco Guardi (Venice, 1973).

Edgar Munhall, ''An Early Acquisition by Henry Clay Frick: Dagnan-Bouveret's Christ and the Disciples at Emmaus,'' Festschrift Reto Conzett (Zurich, 1986), n.p.

Alexandra R. Murphy, Jean-François Millet, ex. cat. Museum of Fine Arts (Boston, 1984).

Alexandra R. Murphy, Monet Unveiled: A New Look at Boston's Paintings, ex. cat. Museum of Fine Arts, (Boston, 1977).

Ellen G. D'Oench, The Conversation Piece: Arthur Devis and His Contemporaries (New Haven, 1980).

Felicity Owen and David Blayney Brown, Collector of Genius: A Life of Sir George Beaumont (New Haven and London, 1988).

Nicholas Penny, ed., Reynolds, ex. cat. Royal Academy of Arts (London, 1986).

Ronald Paulson, Hogarth: His Life, Art, and Times (London, 1971).

Mario Praz, Conversation Pieces A Survey of the Informal Group Portrait in Europe and America (University Park, Pennsylvania and London, 1971).

W. Roberts, ''Mr. H. C. Frick's Collection of Pictures,'' Connoisseur, XXXIV (Nov. 1912), pp. 147-158.

James Byam Shaw, Drawings of Francesco Guardi (London, 1951).

Ellis K. Waterhouse, Gainsborough (London, 1958).

Ellis K. Waterhouse, Reynolds (London, 1941).

William T. Whitley, Thomas Gainsborough (London, 1915).

Acknowledgments

''The Frick Family: A Portrait''
Thanks are extended to Susan Endersbee, Director of the Westmoreland Fayette Historical Society, for information on the Overholt and Frick families. My gratitude is also due to Walter Cooley and Mary Campsey, who verified facts and reviewed the draft of my essay.

Joanne B. Moore

''Clayton: Portrait of the House''
For their assistance I would like to thank: Theodore Dell for advising on the French furniture at Clayton; Alice Frelinghuysen and Catherine Hoover Voorsanger, Metropolitan Museum of Art, for recommendations in the early stages of research; Robert Long for research assistance; Ellen Manyon for research; Jack Thayer, Peabody Museum of Salem, for his thoughts on the Japanese bronze vases; and Janet Zapata, Tiffany & Co. Archives, for information on the company.

Ellen M. Rosenthal

''The Clothing Collection at Clayton''
I would like to thank: Ruth Garfunkle, Norma Hensler, Judith Jerde, and Fame Craig Raisig.

Louise F. Wells